A Parent's Guide To Rais reading for every parent who lives abroad. Dr. Devens answers questions that many people are afraid to ask. He does so with humor, relatable analogies, and research. As a psychologist, he has harnessed a lifetime of wisdom while working with expatriate parents and kids. You won't want to read this just once. Let this book be your constant guide for action and solutions. Yes, it really is that good!

Andrew Hallam
Author of *Millionaire Teacher* and
The Global Expatriate's Guide To Investing:
From Millionaire Teacher to Millionaire Expat

A Parent's Guide to Raising Kids Overseas is a straightforward, practical resource for parents entering into, remaining in, or returning from expatriate living with children. Having attended DoDEA (Department of Defense Education Activity) schools as an elementary student, and later serving as an international school administrator in Singapore, Nepal, Tunisia, and Brazil, I know this life very well. Dr. Devens writes in an insightful and sensible manner. A great resource for our schools and families.

Allan Bredy
Head of School,
American School of Brasilia

Dr. Jeff Devens generously shares straight-up wisdom and insider-trading kind of advice that can only come from someone with decades of hard-earned experience in the trenches with international parents and kids. If you've ever wished you could pick the brain of a well-respected school psychologist, gleaning insights and strategies, and gaining a clear perspective about raising your kids internationally (or anywhere), you need to read this book. It is a labor of love from a person who has seen it all, and who believes deeply in a hopeful outcome for children and families.

Mona Stuart
Former Director of Admissions,
Singapore American School

A Parent's Guide to Raising Kids Overseas is practical, real world, down-to-earth advice encouraging parents of third culture kids to be deliberate in teaching their global, nomad children values that will help them grow into responsible and independent adults. Dr. Devens compassionately addresses a wide range of challenges within a unique expatriate context of privilege and an environment lacking in a supportive, homogenous parenting culture. There isn't an issue that hasn't been addressed. Dr. Devens takes complex concepts—the wicked issues of parenting—and breaks them down into their essential bits, providing concrete, manageable steps, as well as answering the most significant questions parents ask in an FAQ format. He gives parents the nuts and bolts to holistically raising international children to be fully equipped for adulthood.

Dr. Suzanne M. Anderson
Psychotherapist, Registered Social Worker (SG),
Certified Crisis Responder & Trainer (USA)

A Parent's Guide to Raising Kids Overseas

A Parent's Guide to Raising Kids Overseas

International School Psychologist
Dr. Jeff Devens

A Parent's Guide to Raising Kids Overseas
© 2018 by Jeff Devens, Ph.D.

ISBN: 978-1-53750-009-6

Edited by Barbara Farmer
Cover Design by DandD Sol |
https://designers.designcrowd.com/designer/605950/designanddevelopment

To parents, educators, and coaches
who push-n-pull, encourage, and cheer kids on in love.
This book is dedicated to you.

CONTENTS

Foreword xi
Acknowledgements xiii
Introduction 1

1   Welcome Home 7
2   Foundations 19
3   Cornerstones 25
4   Fostering an Attitude of Gratitude 39
5   Questioning Faith 45
6   Moving beyond Self 53
7   The Cost of Comparison 60
8   When Good Enough Is Good Enough 66
9   Doing What Feels Right vs. Doing What Is Right 74
10 How Heartache Produces Hope 80
11 Boundaries 85
12 The Truth of a Lie 92
13 Fully Developed Frontal Lobes: A Parental Dilemma 99
14 Fostering Responsibility and Independence
    in Children and Teens 105
15 From Teenagers to Screenagers 125
16 Game On 134
17 Stressed Out 143
18 Can, Should, Cost: Understanding Testing
    Accommodations for AP/SAT/ACT 152
19 Why Alcohol and Teens Don't Mix 163
20 Know the Signs of Suicide 170
21 A Letter to Husbands 177
22 I'm Not Finished! 185

About the Author 193
Notes 195

FOREWORD

As an international educator, counselor, and psychologist for the last twenty-two years, Dr. Jeff Devens has the experience needed to create this authoritative guide for raising kids outside their home country. Dr. Devens' approach, deeply rooted in his daily work with students, parents, and faculty (as well as in raising two children of his own), is refreshing. Pragmatic, practical, and insightful perspectives dominate every page. He is not reluctant to share his point of view, yet he does so in a manner that encourages parents to consider how their thoughts and actions contribute to raising a child to healthy adulthood.

I am a recently retired, twenty-three-year veteran superintendent of international schools in Saudi Arabia, Singapore, and Dubai. I have seen firsthand the need for—and lack of—readily available information for parents dealing with the challenges associated with international relocation. This book fills that void.

Families who leave the comforts of a familiar environment and move to distant lands will find their challenges are not diminished but different. Raising kids in any environment brings numerous challenges and opportunities, but doing so away from accustomed structures and family support systems adds a unique dimension that is worthy of thoughtful and deliberate attention. While this book speaks directly to those challenges, much of it will resonate with parents no matter what their geographical location may be.

A Parent's Guide to Raising Kids Overseas begins with specific strategies for meeting the challenges associated with an international move. Big-picture issues such as fostering an attitude of gratitude in place of privilege and developing desired morals and values in a culture that may differ greatly from their own are addressed first. Dr. Devens then explains the critical nature of boundaries and guidelines for formulating and enforcing appropriate consequences, including some rules about creating rules. New challenges brought on by our technology-intensive, social-media-driven world are discussed and, interrelated to this,

Dr. Devens reveals the chief causes of teenage stress, explaining why limiting access to technology is necessary as well as addressing assumptions regarding alcohol use among adolescence. What's more, he shares the stages of a crisis response model for dealing with real life heartache and the need for hope.

Dr. Devens' book delivers a comprehensive, compassionate roadmap for parents who are committed to raising independent, responsible young people who will contribute to making this world a better place.

Dr. Brent Mutsch
Former Superintendent
The International Schools Group, Dhahran, Saudi Arabia
Saudi Aramco Schools, Dhahran, Saudi Arabia
Singapore American School, Singapore
The American School of Dubai, United Arab Emirates

ACKNOWLEDGEMENTS

Nanette, my wife and better half, thank you for encouraging me, loving me, giving so much to me, and for being the mother of our children. Can you believe this crazy journey we've been on for nearly twenty-five years—twenty-two of which have been overseas? I thank God when I think of you.

Andrew Hallam, thank you for writing and speaking to those in the international/expatriate community regarding personal finance and stewardship. I truly have appreciated your friendship and encouragement throughout this process. I'm following in your footsteps.

To my editor, Barbara Farmer: It has been such a fun-filled, fantastic process to work with you on this book. Who would have thought a visit by all the Farmers to our cabin last summer would have turned into a writing partnership? How wonderful to reconnect with you and Bret after twenty-plus years. #Collegefriendsareforever!

Cylas and Cora, you two are teaching me more about the meaning and purpose of life than any textbook, speaker, or parenting book ever could, including this one. Thank you for allowing me to guide you, love you, push, and pull you toward adulthood. I love being your dad.

INTRODUCTION

The one constant in life is change…
it is in changing we find purpose.

HERACLITUS (535 BC–475 BC)

"Here we go again!" Tossing his hands in the air in mock surrender, Michael slumped into the chair across from my desk. He'd received news the day before that he and his family would be posted to Vietnam at the end of the year. "How am I going to break this to my family?"

As a father of three (ages sixteen, twelve, and eight), he knew he had a difficult task. This news wouldn't be well received. "We've finally settled in here after two years and now we have to move." He sighed. "And so we begin again."

❧

Each year, thousands of families embark on moves to foreign countries. With increasing globalization, mobility no longer brings isolation, but it does bring change. Kids in the international community are growing up in places like Cambodia while watching American television programs on Netflix, Amazon Prime, and YouTube; gaming with friends in Argentina while living in China; and Skyping weekly with grandparents in Canada while living in Singapore, Japan, or Germany.

My generation (those born between 1966–76, dubbed *Gen X*) didn't grow up with the internet; nor did we experience high mobility. Going overseas truly meant isolation and immersion. Today, the internet has transformed the way kids and parents not only remain connected to those in previous locations but also how they simultaneously make connections with others in their new ones. We are living in a "brave new world."

So, what makes international living unique? For starters, international communities are transient. Many postings are two to three years in duration, after which families move to another

1

post or repatriate. This high level of mobility impacts the development of identity and relationships, both for good and not so good.

Physical separation from extended family, working and traveling parents, and separation from long-term friendships not only affects adults but also their children. Some respond positively by developing early maturation skills such as high levels of verbal and conversational sophistication, richer appreciation of cultural differences, and tolerance. For others, however, these transitions lead to a refusal to connect, criticism of their host culture, and various forms of regression, including behavioral, academic, and physical regression. For some, conflicts between a country's value system and the value system of the parents may cause confusion. Add to this a host of parenting issues (the focus of this book), and one has the makings for exciting parenting times.

However, while families living internationally will come across some unique situations, most of the parenting issues they will face are commonly experienced by most families, regardless of location. I say this to encourage parents around the world (myself included). We are not alone.

WHY THIS BOOK?

This book is not primarily about cultural adjustments, third-culture kids, identity development, or repatriation. There are many organizations and a host of authors who have undertaken useful and valuable works on these topics. The focus of this book is on raising kids in the context of these differences.

To be sure, I'll be touching on the topics of transitions and identity; however, my purpose in writing this book is to address day-to-day common issues of parenting and raising kids overseas. From the outset, I acknowledge I am a Westerner (USA), attempting to write a book for an international audience. I recognize I too hold cultural biases even with twenty-two years of international experience as a school psychologist, counselor, and educator. These experiences have influenced the ways in which I work, write, and think about kids and families.

One of the many unique features of international communities is the varying norms rooted in different cultural traditions that students and their families represent. Unlike schools in monocultural settings, international schools may be comprised of families representing well over fifty different countries. In most cases, this adds a dynamic mix of cultural awareness and tolerance. Sometimes, however, this can also contribute to a feeling of cultural confusion. Unfamiliar religious practices, differing values of other parents, and cultural traditions of host countries can be both confusing and conflicting.

International and Department of Defense Education Activity (DoDEA) often takes on the role of surrogate family. As you know, schools aren't attended solely for academic studies. Commonly, there's more going on at school and after school than during class hours. Schools often serve as the hub for the community. This is a primary reason I so appreciate working in educational institutions abroad. I've had the fortunate pleasure of working with, and living among, some fantastic people. I've learned much about myself, taken down cultural stereotypes, constructed others (sadly), and worked with some amazing kids, families, and colleagues along the way.

WHAT TYPES OF SCHOOLS COMMONLY EXIST ABROAD?

International Schools

A recent report from the International School Consultancy Group (ISC) notes there are 8,924 international schools teaching over 4.85 million students.[1] ISC predicts by 2026, this number will be over 11,000 schools serving 6.3 million students.[2]

The majority of children in these schools have parents who work for multinational corporations or nongovernmental organizations (NGOs). They have high levels of educational attainment and are part of two-parent families. The parents place high academic expectations on their children and are often willing to pay for a high level of educational service for them.

International and Department of Defense schools are often the first options of consideration for families. These schools are designed to support the educational needs of kids and families as they move from one country to another. Many offer educational experiences similar to what might be found in their country of passport, including curriculum, learning standards, and educational supports. However, depending on the location of the school, resources and staffing may be limited.

International schools have different models of learning, depending on their founding charters. For example, many schools offer an International Baccalaureate (IB) program for students between three and nineteen years old, with an emphasis on developing intellectual, personal, emotional, and social skills. With over 3,881 schools in 148 countries, IB's aim is to offer a seamless educational experience for students and families who transition from country to country. Other international schools operating independently of IB also offer a quality educational experience. In some cases, schools tailor learning so students can transition back to their country of passport.

Department of Defense Education Activity Schools

Not long after the end of WWII, the United States military established schools for the children of its servicemen and women stationed overseas. The Department of Defense Dependent Schools (DoDDS), located overseas, and the Department of Defense Domestic Dependent Elementary and Secondary Schools (DDESS), located in the United States, merged in 1994 to form the Department of Defense Education Activity (DoDEA).

The Department of Defense Education Activity operates 191 schools in fourteen districts located in twelve foreign countries, seven states, Guam, and Puerto Rico. There are approximately 86,000 students (or 172,000 parents) that are part of DoDEA.[3] The intent of such schools is to provide an extension of US-based education and practices to those serving in the military and who have dependents.

HOW IS THIS BOOK ORGANIZED?

A Parent's Guide to Raising Kids Overseas is divided into several sections or themes. While not necessarily meant to be read from cover to cover, there's nothing wrong with doing so. Throughout the book, you'll note similar themes repeated. This redundancy is intentional as an aid for building retention. Some chapters in the book have specific connections to international living while others are essential nuts-and-bolts of foundational parenting.

At the end of each chapter is the FAQs (Frequently Asked Questions) section addressing questions commonly asked by parents. While I'll provide plenty of "I believe" and "This is what I think about X issue" answers, most of the content is based on day-to-day experiences that families, kids, educators, and administrators have shared with me throughout my practice. Their stories influence my writing, and it's their life experiences I'll be sharing. The names and identifying details of individuals mentioned in this book have been changed to protect their privacy, but the events are as real as it gets when raising kids overseas.

For those seeking timely, relevant, practical, and proven advice from the trenches on raising children aboard, this book is for you. It is also for those stepping into the international scene for the first time. Observing the wisdom and experiences of those who've gone before us is a primary way to learn and prepare for the future. It can hopefully help you avoid some of the not-so-good experiences that others have encountered in the past. If you understand and incorporate these principles into your parenting paradigm, you will increase your likelihood of raising kids who will be ready to step into adulthood with the tools necessary for independence. And remember, enjoy the journey.

ॐ

If you would like more information regarding conference presentations, speaking engagements, teacher/parent workshops, or parenting consultations, please contact me via email or Twitter.

Email: Overseasparenting@gmail.com
Twitter: https://twitter.com/overseasparent

1

Welcome Home

*It's not because I have received a better education,
but a broader education. I can tell my cousins [that] Georgia
is not only the name of a state but also the name of a country.
I've had more of an international experience, and this
has significantly changed my outlook.*

KATIE, AGE 17

According to your circadian rhythm, you should be awake. The only problem is, it's 2:30 in the morning on this side of the world. Sitting on the floor of your unfurnished apartment, attempting to assemble an IKEA bookshelf with the semi-functional tools provided, you wonder aloud, "Is this ever going to feel like home?"

I remember my initial impressions of our first international move. In the span of twenty-four hours, we went from a sunny day in clean, efficient, predictable Minnesota, USA, to the wonderful zaniness that is Beijing, China. Talk about contrasts!

It was 1996, but walking through the airport in Beijing felt like we'd passed through a wormhole and been transported to a bygone era. The military-green paint that peeled off the airport walls contrasted sharply with the bright red communist star on the ceiling, and we knew we weren't among the familiar in any sense of the word.

What began as a two-year overseas experience has grown into a twenty-two-year lifestyle. Living in China, Saudi Arabia, and most recently Singapore has afforded us life-enriching experiences—experiences that have forever changed our lives.

๛

For some of you, this is your first international posting or deployment. You might even have had to search Google Maps to locate your new address. Others of you are seasoned veterans. Your current posting is but one of several you and your family have called home. In either case, there's a series of transition stages that both kids and parents will go through. In regard to these stages, I am indebted to David Pollock and Ruth Van Reken for their seminal work on understanding the transition process, as noted in their book, *Third Culture Kids: Growing Up Among Worlds.*[1] It's a must-read for international families.

Being aware of these stages can reassure you that what you and your family are going through is normal.

Stage 1: Settled

This describes your status before your move. For children, this means they are attending school, have a predictable, established routine with a peer group, and are engaged in the community. They are responsive and responsible. Adults too have set patterns in place: their commute to work, the stores they frequent, and even their favorite coffee shop. In short, life is predictable.

Stage 2: Leaving

At some point, a decision is made to move. This decision may provide several months prior notice, or it could require a move within a few short weeks. Leaving is a time of saying goodbye and disengaging. Kids and adults experience a range of emotional responses during this period, including excitement, joy, anticipation, anxiety, denial, anger, resentment, bargaining, sadness, and loss.

Stage 3: Honeymoon

Upon arriving in an unfamiliar cultural context, the common tendency is to look for what is familiar and establish a routine. It's also a time when others extend themselves to welcome new families. Kids tend to feel pretty good and function at a high level. The honeymoon stage typically lasts ten minutes to two months.

Stage 4: Disorientation

For many, the more they interact with the host culture, the more they become disoriented and melancholy. Two primary reasons for this are the loss of social support systems (friends, family, community) and the lack of predictability. People may experience a range of emotional responses: mourning the loss of friends, feeling isolated, exaggerating problems and behaviors, feeling tired and grumpy, judging the host culture negatively, and refusing to connect. It's not uncommon for kids to want to stay tethered to friends in their previous location/posting and not make new friends. Holing up in their bedrooms, they may spend significant amounts of time communicating with their old friends online. They may also struggle academically during the first quarter or semester of school. During this stage, parents encounter the most difficult issues related to the move. A holiday, time of year, birthday, or another significant event can trigger strong emotional responses. This period usually lasts from one to six months and can sometimes flare up anew when the family returns home for their first long holiday.

Stage 5: Recovery and Adjustment

As kids continue to interact with the new culture, they begin to incorporate their understanding of themselves, school, friends, and so forth, and start to feel at home. Their functioning levels typically return to normal, sometimes even to higher than normal levels because of all they have learned about themselves and the world. The benefits of this include increased social maturity, a broader worldview, less prejudice, and a greater cultural and religious tolerance.

A complicating factor to these transition stages is that each of your family members will go through them at different times. There may even be periods when kids vacillate between them. What's important to keep in mind is that what they are experiencing is normal and part of the transition process.

FAQs

When should we tell our kids we're moving? The most advantageous time to inform your children would be when you know moving is a strong likelihood. Depending on their age, children will experience a host of normal childhood responses: excitement, denial, withdrawal, anger, joy, and so on. Kids, especially younger ones, often mimic the emotional state of their parents. It's important to help children process the various feelings that encompass saying goodbye and moving on. For instance, feelings of anxiety often overwhelm kids when they contemplate fitting into a new school community and unfamiliar culture.

Keep in mind the adjustment phase begins before the actual physical move. During this time, it is not uncommon to note a drop in academic performance, an increase in peer difficulties, and regression of behaviors. Anticipating changes and addressing your child's concerns are important front-end work.

When's the best time to move? In most cases, the best time to move is when kids begin a new school term, specifically at the start of the school year. During this time, schools devote considerable resources to support new students and families. If you're new to international or Department of Defense schools, you'll quickly come to understand that these communities are transient. As such, kids and families move in and out of these schools at a higher rate than one finds in their home country. It is not uncommon for 25 percent or more of students to be new each year. Knowing that he's not the only new kid may be comforting to your child. As a general rule, if you can finish out the school year in your current post, do so before moving on.

How can I help prepare my kids for the move? Going online and searching out the school and culture is a good starting point to prepare your whole family. Look at the school website, courses, schedule, graduation requirements, and so on. Many schools post YouTube videos of the school and community. If you have an opportunity to visit the school before your family arrives, put together a video for the kids. Include photos of prospective houses, activities, eateries, and outside activities.

The key is to create a context for the new setting.

What school records will my child's new school require? Most schools will review the last three years of academic records. You can gather these from your child's current school. Every school keeps a running record of a student's academic progress, often known as their *cumulative folder*. Quarter, semester, and final marks, along with teacher comments and any standardized assessments, are of particular importance. If your child has had any psychoeducational evaluations or is presently receiving academic support (IEP or 504 plans), you will need current copies of these documents (within the last two years).

Many overseas schools do not have extensive academic support programs. Thus, they will need to review your child's case history to determine whether they can accommodate his or her academic, social, or emotional needs. Sadly, some parents knowingly withhold this information to gain admission. When the school does find out—and they will—they may rescind the offer of admission. Parents, be honest with this information. It does your child no good to be in a school that doesn't provide the services and supports they need to be successful.

My child was doing well academically at their previous school, but now they are struggling. What's going on here? Make allowances for kids who appear out-of-sync academically, at least during the first quarter (nine weeks) of school. It is also important to understand the demographics of the school population. In your child's previous school, they may have been a good student, but by international standards, they may be academically average. The international community often has a larger percentage of high-level academics due to demographics: Most students come from intact, middle- to upper-class, well-educated families with stable support systems in place. As such, academic rigor is a foundational part of the makeup of these families and schools. If your child is an average student based on standardized measures, they may be below average compared to peers at their international school. If they were above average domestically, they might be average internationally, and so on.

If your child isn't making consistent progress, speak with

their teachers. Be sure to talk with the electives teachers (physical education, music, art) as well. These teachers can often provide information related to the social-emotional aspects of your child's situation and adjustment, which are perhaps more important than academic aspects during the transition phase.

Should we keep our current home? A life lived out of a suitcase for eight weeks during school holidays becomes tiring. Many international families purchase homes and return to them during extended school breaks. This investment shouldn't be considered purely financial. It is great if you can rent your place while you're abroad, but in many cases, this may not be possible. My advice is to make the financial investment for the gain in connectedness and community, especially if you are uncertain how long you will be out of the country. Most postings are two- to three-year terms. Knowing this, many families plan to return home. If this doesn't describe your situation, then selling and deciding to buy somewhere else may be a better option.

To convince my child to move, I had to promise we would go back to visit the place we are currently living during midterm break. Was this a good idea? Yes and no. If your kids are well adjusted and have come to understand that transitions are a natural part of the international experience, then offering them the opportunity to reconnect with old friends can demonstrate to them that you recognize the importance of friends in their lives.

However, if the kids are refusing to connect with new peers, this can be a real drain on the family. In some cases, children finally begin to settle into the routine of living in a new post, only to start the process all over again after they visit their old friends. Each family is unique; parents should keep in mind how their kids handle transitions before making concessions.

Why isn't my child connecting or engaging with peers? When children enter a new environment, they look for what's familiar. Kids thrive—as do adults—on routine, predictability, and relationships. When they don't find these, a host of negative emotional and physiological responses can be set in motion. For example, a colleague of mine moved to a new posting but didn't take the helper/maid who had worked with the family for six years. For their six-year-old child, the helper was a relative, a third parent in effect, who was no longer there. The result was a regression of behaviors, including bed-wetting, that lasted several weeks until the child had mourned the loss.

Transitions may affect children in a myriad of ways: withdrawal, rebelliousness, anxiety, clinginess, night terrors, stunted academic progress, little physical activity, and more. To some degree, these reactions and responses are to be expected. The difficulty occurs when the behavior becomes persistent (typically lasting more than twelve weeks). In such cases, it's vitally important to speak with your child's teachers or counselor, explaining the specifics of what you're noting. Adjustment to a new post can take eighteen to thirty-six weeks. Most kids, however, make the necessary changes and return to normal or higher levels of functioning within the first eighteen weeks.

I want to reemphasize the importance of routine; this can't be overstated. Establish a routine as soon as you can, including mealtime, bedtimes, school, sports, and other extracurricular activities.

What if my child refuses to connect? Refusing to connect does happen, and when it does, it is taxing for the entire family. I remember working with a family who had a senior in high school (age seventeen). The new location was the last place he wanted to be, even though he had willingly agreed to move there several months prior. Initially, he refused to go to school. When he did finally show up, he refused to do any schoolwork. He continued to demand a return "home," even though there was no one there to look after him. As the year progressed, he bargained, threatened, and harassed his parents. They eventually decided Mom would go back home and allow him to finish out his senior year in the United States, while Dad remained overseas.

When this potential exists, it is important for parents to ask themselves one essential question: Is there any chance whatsoever my child could return to the previous post or home? If the answer is "maybe," or "we'll see," and your child does not want to move, you can expect conflict. It is far better to say no from the outset and deal with that conflict than to throw out a bribe that you know isn't a real option. Parents often make decisions with which their kids disagree. Sadly, in the above case, the message this young man walked away with was that his needs were more important than the family's.

There may be extenuating circumstances, of course, when it is better to remain in your current post to allow your children to finish the school year or to graduate before moving on. If your child is in the last two years of high school, as far as it depends on you, I strongly encourage you to remain at your current post/job. However, if this cannot happen and your child wishes to stay on at their current school, other possibilities may be available. Your teen could live with another family, could board at the school if that service is available, or one parent may remain while the working spouse moves on for the school year. Some families make this difficult decision each year. Keep in mind, the decision may be further complicated when more than one child is in the home.

Should we allow our son to continue communicating with his old friends even when he doesn't seem to be connecting with his peers at the new school? With the advent of Facebook, Twitter, Skype, Instagram, Snapchat, SMS, and other social media, it's difficult to keep kids from being in contact with old friends. In fact, it's quite common—and healthy—for children to form lifelines with former classmates, using them as a base of support and security during the transition. Difficulty arises when they refuse to connect with the host culture, school, and new peers. Even with this possibility, however, I wouldn't remove or restrict access to old friends unless they were a negative influence. As your children engage with peers in their new school, a routine will develop (through sports, clubs, sleepovers, etc.), and they'll see that forming new friendships doesn't mean betraying old ones.

Note: It's important for kids to have a routine in their sleep patterns. Sometimes teens will want to remain in contact with old peers even though there is a twelve-hour time-zone difference. Parents may need to help them regulate the amount of time they spend online.

Our first year abroad was great. The kids adjusted, we adjusted; overall we had a great experience. Sadly, when we returned home for our school holiday (furlough, break), no one seemed to care about our experiences. Worse still, people thought we were bragging. This wasn't our intention. What's going on here? For others to make sense of your international experiences, they may need a reference point. It's not so much that people aren't interested as it is they don't have a context in which to frame your stories. Walking the treetops in the Amazon rainforest, viewing the pyramids of Egypt, or taking in the grandeur of the Great Wall of China are commonplace occurrences for many international families. So too is witnessing abject poverty, pollution, and lack of resources in many developing countries. Those with limited international experience may perceive your travel knowledge as bragging (as, indeed, some folks may do.) As a result, after a few years of international living, many stop talking about their experiences, choosing instead to compartmentalize this portion of their lives.

If you're new to the international scene, I encourage you to provide opportunities for your extended family to visit. Doing so will go a long way in keeping you connected with those back home and creating a context for your loved ones of where you're living overseas. Invite them to personally feel the heat, smell the spices, and sense the undercurrents of the culture. If this isn't feasible, consider writing a blog or posting photos and videos on Facebook and other forms of interactive media to share your experiences.

It seems every year my child has to make new friends, and we aren't the ones moving on. How can I help? This is an often-overlooked aspect of high-mobility communities. Among international communities, there's a segment of the student population that doesn't move on, but these kids regularly experience the loss of friendships over the years. Having to form new relationships each year can be just as frustrating for them as it is for those who have moved on. Saying goodbye to best friends on a yearly basis can take its toll. These kids will also be dealing with grief and loss and may experience a dip in academic performance, motivation, and overall mood. You can help your child by recognizing the stages of grief—denial, anger, bargaining, depression, acceptance—acknowledging the feelings, and providing healthy outlets for them to express their emotions. Allowing your children to stay connected through social media can also be a positive thing.

It's not unusual for kids to reconnect over the summer or holiday breaks. Times like these help strengthen good relationships. In many cases when the kids are good friends, so are the parents. These opportunities to get together can be just as important for parents as they are for kids.

The reality is, they will feel loss, they will feel pain, and they will need time to go through the grieving process.

After five years abroad, we told our kids we were going home. They broke down in tears, protesting, "We are home!" What are we to do now? Most expatriates and military families will return to their country of passport. It is not uncommon for families to work abroad two or three years, repatriate two or three years, then move on to another overseas posting. These experiences can be wonderfully enriching and gut wrenching at the same time.

What often happens, for both kids and adults is, over time, "home" is no longer limited to a particular country. Rather, home is comprised of a series of relationships, experiences, and encounters with others from around the world. In this sense, kids and adults have become global citizens. Their understanding of the world has been forever changed, often for the positive, because of these experiences. The US government takes great strides to ensure military families remain connected to American culture. Even so, one cannot help being impacted by living abroad.

If your family has spent considerable time (three to four years) living outside your country of passport, you can bet your kids see the world and their place in it through markedly different lenses than they did before. And so will you. For example, if you're forty years old and have lived overseas the past decade, this amounts to 25 percent of your life. If you have a fifteen-year-old, those same ten years amount to 66 percent of his or her life. Despite a passport that identifies them as a citizen of the United States, Korea, Canada, Australia, or India, they are going to view themselves, or be seen by same age peers, as different. One student told me he felt like a counterfeit. He has all the outside appearances (clothes, accent, culinary preferences, and so on) of an American but very few traditional American experiences.

Parents, when you return to your country of passport or move on to another posting, anticipate adjustments. You and your children will be going through a cycle of transition. The degree of difficulty experienced will differ from person to person, but the sequence of stages is generally consistent. Your children will need help adjusting to life back home. You may need to speak with teachers, coaches, and other caring adults to help their transition. Just as moving to a new posting requires a transition, so will moving back to your country of passport be an adjustment and will take time.

Our company (or military liaison) arranged for us to move overseas but has offered little follow-through with helping us settle. Being thousands of miles away from home in a foreign country makes us feel like they only care about the work they can get out of us at the expense of family. What are we to do? International companies, as a whole, do a lousy job of follow-through when it comes to helping families settle into a new posting. To be fair, there are a few companies that have dedicated resources for helping the family unit transition. Such companies understand a settled home life makes for a highly productive employee. To these companies, I say, *bravo!*

Companies that do not offer extended settling-in services are throwing away hundreds of thousands of dollars over the course of an employee's tenure. Failing to understand the importance of family dynamics and adjustment issues is a primary factor in low work performance and shortened work life for international employees. I have had countless discussions with parents about the lack of support they have received while abroad; many cite this as a primary reason for repatriating.

As far as military support for families, it's important to connect early with your sponsor. Make sure you ask specific questions regarding life on the compound or community, schooling, safety, travel, food, and medical resources. Ask about ongoing support upon arrival. Go online and look at the schools. What services do they provide, what curriculum do they use, and how do they integrate learning styles with kids who may indicate the presence of a learning gap? These are all critical questions to sort out ahead of time.

If you're thinking of moving overseas, make sure you understand the costs—financial and otherwise. Companies hiring you or your spouse will expect significant amounts of time dedicated to this role. Frequent travel, long working hours, and high pressures are but a few of the costs commonly associated with expatriate life. Be sure to weigh these factors against your family's needs before accepting an offer.

I've been moved overseas to work. While I realized much would be required before I started this job, I didn't fully appreciate how much time away from family it would require. What should I do now? I have met with scores of families arriving overseas for their first posting or deployment that did not realize the demands that would be placed on the working spouse and, subsequently, the family. This work often consists of frequent travel, long hours, and weekend obligations. It seems little can be done to find time for family needs.

Sometimes, circumstances are not within a parent's control when it comes to work. Other times, the choices we make are just that, choices. We choose to enlist or climb the corporate ladder one more rung, believing we're doing it for the kids. There are times when parents make sacrifices for the family, but other times they sacrifice their family. I don't believe this has to be an either-or proposition, but at times, that is the case.

For those on active duty, your deployment is a term. Re-enlistment is a choice. Signing on for additional years of service is a decision that should be made by husband and wife. Once the choice has been jointly made, the trailing partner should not continue to argue or protest the long hours or months that their partner is away from home. The time to argue is during the decision phase, not after. When arguing like this occurs after the fact, it erodes the relationship and does psychological harm to the family.

2

Foundations

Home is the bottom line of life, the anvil
upon which attitudes and convictions
are hammered out—the single most
influential force in our earthly existence.
No price tag can adequately reflect its value.

CHARLES R. SWINDOLL

"This is where it all begins," Jerry said, and I knew we weren't going to like hearing the rest of the news. Nanette, my wife and better half, and I had completed our first year working overseas and were on vacation in North Dakota (USA), our *home*. With money saved from our first year of work at the International School of Beijing, we were looking to purchase a lake cabin.

Our friend Jerry, a salt-of-the-earth, cross between a lone cowboy and Mr. Fix-it, had different thoughts than we did about the one were looking at. By trade, Jerry was a cement worker, laying home foundations for well over thirty years. He took us to the basement of the home and, pulling back the basement carpet, revealed several jagged cracks in the concrete from one side of the floor to the other. Scratching his head and sounding apologetic, he said, "This house looks beautiful from upstairs, but it's down here that matters most." Pointing to the ceiling above, he went on, "What happens with the foundation will ultimately reveal itself up there."

He was right. The kitchen above had a slope in the floor, one I had overlooked as cosmetic until Jerry confirmed otherwise. It mattered not what the bedroom, kitchen, or bathrooms looked like when the foundation of the home wasn't secure, stable, or dependable. "It's from here," Jerry said, pointing to the foundation, "that the rest of the house is built." His sage advice saved us from making a costly mistake.

> ❧

Jerry's pearls of wisdom spoken some twenty years ago still ring true as I work with families in crisis. Listening to their stories of heartache, I often wonder what went into their foundation. When the proverbial winds howl, rains fall, and the storms of life occur—and they will—foundations must provide stability and security.

Solid foundations preserve and protect. From the moment your child arrived, you've laid foundational stones upon which their life and learning is built. So, what are the stones forming the bedrock of your family? As you delve into the remaining chapters of this book, I want to be very clear about one point: *Don't leave this responsibility with the schools your children attend.*

I write these words respectfully and humbly as a psychologist, educator, and parent. While schools commonly have a set of guiding principles, sometimes termed *values* or *cornerstones*, how these principles are implemented varies markedly. In school settings, much of the implementation is left to individual teachers. In most cases, your children will be fortunate to work with excellent educators who are kind, caring, and compassionate. However, when it comes to questions regarding foundations, I assure you, teachers struggle with the outworking of what this means—even in their own lives. Foundations must be laid in the home. This is difficult but necessary work if parents are to raise healthy, responsible, independent kids.

George Barna, pollster and author of more than forty books regarding American culture, notes that in the past twenty years, the ignoring or deemphasizing of foundations has produced five outcomes in culture:

- the absence of a shared vision of the future;
- confusion regarding appropriate values for decision making;
- the elimination of a sense of the common good;

- the deterioration of respectful dialogue and the fruitful exchange of competing ideas; and
- the abandonment of moral character and personal decency.[1]

In many respects, what is happening in the United States is a microcosm of what is taking place internationally. When parents abdicate these responsibilities, it doesn't mean their child's foundation won't be laid. It will. The question is, what will go into it?

The answers to building a healthy foundation aren't as simple as "spend time with your kids," but that's the starting point. Foundations are formed in the day-to-day. What are you doing to impart values in the lives of your children on a daily basis? On the other side of the coin, what are your long-term parenting goals for supporting and sustaining your child's foundation?

For example, in our home, one of our foundation stones is modeling to our son and daughter what realistic love in the form of our marriage looks like—warts and all. Sadly, the word *love* has been bastardized by the media and culture so much that it's viewed primarily as emotional or sexual or both. Yet love entails so much more. Our children won't understand the differences between genuine love and entertainment-style love unless our marriage models otherwise. If we fail to cultivate or if we violate love, the cost will be a marring or distortion of what it means to love another. The outworking of our marriage provides the framework for our children to help them understand what to look for in a potential mate seventy years from now when they are allowed to marry. (Okay, maybe forty). Contrast this type of love with the media's version, namely a teenage girl and a 104-year-old vampire,[2] and you begin to understand just what parents are up against. Love is but one of many foundational stones in our family.

Schools will do their best to model foundational beliefs or core values; however, how beliefs and values work themselves out is a function of the home. Some readers may be wondering how these foundational experiences differ for international kids compared to the kids they know in the culture back home? The answer comes in the experiences they'll have. In many cases, these will be markedly different from peers who don't experience life abroad. If you choose to raise kids overseas, they *will be* exposed to worldviews that differ radically from what you're accustomed. This is a unique and fantastic feature of raising kids overseas; it is also a potential pitfall.

Your children need your guidance to understand what they ought to believe or, at minimum, what you desire of them. Don't leave this task to others. I cannot overstate that point! This includes your children's teachers. Your kids are depending on *you* to help them sort out what is right and wrong regarding morals, values, cultural practices, and beliefs—aka, foundations.

As I write this, I already hear critics saying, "Who are you to judge?" My response: "*I am a parent.* It's my job to equip my kids with critical thinking, including the ability to make judgments." I trust and I hope you feel the same regarding your children. Parents must not abdicate this most important of responsibilities. While parents and kids should be open to growth and change, there will be facets of life—regardless of a country's cultural norms, pop media, social practices, or even what schools promote—that you will oppose.

FAQs

Why all this talk about foundations? Foundations matter because all of life is built upon them, and in an international community, you can bet there will be competing worldviews. For example, in my present school, students represent more than forty-five countries. Families have a broad array of religious beliefs, values, and practices. This is indicative of many international and Department of Defense schools. Knowing other children will influence your children (in many wonderful ways, I might add), how will you make concerted efforts to ensure your values and beliefs are passed on to your children? As politically incorrect as this may read, you don't want everything in your child's host culture, school, or community to become part of their foundation. There will be clear distinctions, and they will matter.

Why don't schools just focus on academics? To a large degree, foundations are understood in the context of learning. Schools have a unique challenge: They must attempt to foster a set of values, practices, and beliefs, while at the same time teaching language arts, math, music, physical education, science, social studies, and more. Schools provide students with a cursory understanding of differing worldview foundations, and they must balance educating without indoctrinating. Sometimes schools do a great job with this, and sometimes not so much. Hari Raya Puasa, Deepavali, Hari Raya Haji, Thanksgiving, Christmas, Chinese New Year, Easter, and Vesak Day are but a few of the holidays teachers educate students about. Understanding the reasons for such celebrations is all about understanding cultural foundations.

What if I don't want to expose my children to different cultures? If you want to ensure your child is exposed only to your cultural beliefs and practices, then I advise against moving abroad. Contact with other cultures is an inherent and integral part of the international experience. Some parents do find this unsettling because they find themselves questioning their own beliefs in the presence of differing cultures. With developing cognitive skills, teens will also question and challenge parental assumptions regarding their foundational beliefs. Sometimes parents assume their beliefs are under attack. The reality, however, is kids are searching for truth. The questions parents contend with aren't so much cultural as much as they are about truth in the context of culture. If our beliefs are primarily the outworking of culture and practice and not grounded in truth, then conflicts will abound. Parents, what do you believe when it comes to matters of values and faith, and why do you believe them? Clear answers to these questions can strengthen your child's foundation. Vague and uncertain answers—or no answers at all—can erode any foundational groundwork already laid.

What role does character education have in shaping foundations? When a school has a shared vision of which character attributes are important for students to embody, the entire culture of that school can be affected in wonderfully positive ways. The challenge schools face in working with a diverse student/family population is finding common ground. For example, an Australian school located in the Middle East may have markedly different beliefs regarding the role of women than those of the culture around them. In such differing geographic and cultural settings, how do schools find common ground on this topic when speaking to a diverse student/parent body? Is common ground even possible? Such questions must be addressed by both schools and parents. Conflicting signals lead to confusion and uncertainty for students and parents alike. I found this to be the case while working at an American school during our term in Saudi Arabia. Try teaching the subject of women's suffrage in a US history course, as I did, to a group of tenth-grade girls (fifteen to sixteen years old), who returned home each evening to cultural practices fundamentally different from those just taught in their school.

What do you believe is the most important foundational stone in a child's life? Much of what we believe about ourselves and others is derived from faith. I'll be unpacking what I mean by the term (faith) in chapter five. For now, let me summarize by saying that what we believe about faith—who or what we put our trust in—may be the most important thing about ourselves. It is from faith that one derives purpose, meaning, and ultimately worth. Let me emphasize again: all of us invest in something or someone beyond ourselves to find value and meaning in life. This is true even to those who profess no faith.

3

Cornerstones

Character cannot be developed in ease and quiet.
Only through experience of trial and suffering can the soul
be strengthened, vision cleared, ambition inspired,
and success achieved.

HELEN KELLER

Each Friday morning, the high school counseling team and I meet in my office. Ten people cram into a small but comfortable space. Our purpose: debriefing the past four days of school. Common questions include: "Which kids are dealing with mental health issues that we need to be aware of?" "What referrals do we need to consider for them?" "Do their friends and parents need support?"

One week, however, the question was different: "Are we doing enough to educate the students about racism?"

The question stemmed from a series of ongoing discussions regarding culture, teens, international students, and ignorance. What followed was a robust discussion regarding ways in which we could further educate students, faculty, and the community. More importantly, we wondered which role(s) the school ought to play in the process and which role(s) parents should assume. The lines of demarcation were anything but clear. What was obvious however was that additional work needed to be done.

Character and character development in the lives of children are increasingly being relegated to a significant part of what schools are expected to do. While there is value in schools sharing a common vision when it comes to character, historically this was a primary function of parents.

❧

Abraham Lincoln once described character as a tree and reputation as the shadow it casts. Character, however, is much more than reputation. Reputation has to do with what others perceive you to be. Character is what we see within ourselves. This isn't to suggest that character is innate—it isn't. Character must be developed. That begins in the home, and it grows as a result of the day-to-day conversations and interactions among family members.

A school's role ought to be one of reinforcing positive character qualities; however, in an international community, this can be difficult. My goal in writing this chapter isn't so much to educate as it is to inform parents of what I've experienced over the years. It is my hope that the character traits discussed here will become part of the ongoing work parents undertake in the home.

This chapter will discuss five essential cornerstones: honesty, responsibility, respect, fairness, and compassion.

HONESTY

Language is, by its very nature, a social phenomenon. With it, we convey meaning, provide insight, articulate emotions, and lie. Social psychologist Dr. Robert Feldman of the University of Massachusetts found ordinary people lie, on average, two times every ten minutes. He notes, "People lie for all sorts of reasons, including puffing themselves up, tearing others down, to avoid hurting others' feelings, to protect their friends, and to coerce people." Lying, says Dr. Feldman, is simply the way the social world operates. Dr. Feldman concluded his research noting, "Since trust is what lubricates relationships and since honesty is what produces trust, we are better off if honesty is the norm."[1]

Modeling and Teaching Integrity

In the home, parents take the lead when it comes to cultivating an atmosphere of honesty, setting the standards their children must follow. To a great extent, a child's ability to be a person of integrity rises and falls in direct proportion to how parents deal with this in their lives. We must understand that lying is not always overt. Often it takes a more subtle form by shading or stretching the truth. Two common forms of "truth stretching" that occur in the home are breaking promises and committing slander.

Breaking Promises. Giving one's word (promise) isn't a trite expression. Rather, giving and keeping one's word speaks volumes regarding a person's character. Teaching kids to honor their word starts with parents who honor theirs. If you make a promise to your spouse or children, keep it. Saying "maybe" or "we'll see," all the while knowing you have no intention of following through, is lying. It's better, albeit sometimes more difficult, to be honest enough to say "no" or "I can't." Granted, there are times when a promise is made but, because of extenuating circumstances, cannot be kept. In such situations, take the time to explain why and ask for forgiveness. Similarly, if your child promises to do something, make sure they understand the implications of what they are saying before they commit. Surprisingly, it's not uncommon for kids to be cajoled into making promises by parents who are desperate to see change. However, doing so when the child does not understand what it means to give one's word (consequences and all) is a sure recipe for failure.

Giving one's word extends well beyond the home. When your child expresses an interest in being part of a sports team or other extracurricular group (musical production, chess or robotics club, etc.), help them understand the commitment they are potentially making. Quitting after two weeks because the activity is no longer fun shouldn't be an option. Require them to finish out the season, regardless of whether they enjoy it or not. Why? Because making a commitment isn't about feelings; it's about behavior. Next season, if they don't want to participate in the activity, that may be fine. For now, they've made a commitment to the other kids and the sponsor or coach. Others are depending on them to keep their word through the season, even if they don't feel like it. If they want to have a poor attitude (by the way, this is the first tactic kids employ to remove themselves from commitment and consequences), address it, but don't allow them to renege on their word.

Committing Slander. *Webster's* defines slander in two forms: 1) "The utterance of false charges or misrepresentations which defame and damage another's reputation." 2) "A false and defamatory oral statement about a person."[2] Slander causes tension, hostility, and conflict. It separates families and friends, tears apart communities, and destroys people's reputations. Slander distorts the way others perceive a person and colors one's view in such a way it's often impossible to expunge. If your child commits slander, you must address this. Not doing so in effect condones what has been said. Often, however, a parent's tendency is not to say anything because we've engaged in this practice ourselves and saying something makes us feel like a hypocrite. Listen, it is never too late to make a change, to forge a new path, and to commit to being a person of integrity when it comes to how we speak about others. Your kids need your guidance and authenticity in order to understand what slandering means.

Dealing with Integrity Issues

What about the times when we do need to speak to another's behaviors or actions? They need to know that telling the truth doesn't always pay but telling a lie always costs. A child who habitually stretches the truth or is otherwise dishonest will carry those tendencies into adulthood. So what is the best way to address honesty issues?

Address It Face-to-Face. Conversations dealing with behaviors or actions must take place when the other person is physically present. There is so much more being communicated than the words we use. People watch body language, listen to tone, and look for eye contact. We demonstrate our passion, concern, and feelings in body language, not words alone. This is partly why using social media to communicate conflict is such a bad idea, not to mention it's a cowardly and ineffective way of handling problems. Type in a few words, hit send, and the relationship is over. Social media must not be the go-to when it comes to addressing conflict.

Address the Issue Privately. Conflict shouldn't be used as an opportunity to air issues in public. When an issue of contention is addressed publicly, those around will often take sides. This occurs when one or both parties pitches a proverbial tent, makes camp, and invites others to join. Doing this does not bring about positive resolution. Instead, it hurts people's feelings and escalates tension. It is best to avoid this and keep the focus on the issues.

State Facts without Exaggeration. Avoid words such as, *always*, *never*, *all the time*, and *everyone*. These terms leave little room for a person to justify or explain their actions.

Seek Reconciliation. No one likes to be corrected, especially in matters related to our speech. Having our speech corrected can be more painful than having our actions corrected, because "out of the abundance of the heart [the] mouth speaks."[3] In other words, it can be more painful because we are showing what is truly in our heart. Similarly, actions are sometimes more easily forgiven than words. Regardless, not addressing these issues—whether in word or in deed—causes seeds of bitterness and anger to flourish.

Reconciliation—the act of restoring friendly relations—isn't a comfortable process. It involves searching one's own heart first, owning any actions and words that offended, and attempting to make things right by another. If you are in the wrong, don't let the matter go unattended. Address it with the offended person, and do so with humility, seeking forgiveness.

To be sure there may be situations where others refuse your attempts at reconciliation; however, you can't own this. If you have attempted to make things right between you and another person and they've refused to accept your heartfelt attempt, so be it. Going forward, commit to what you said you were or were not going to do. Let your future actions and words be the testimony of a changed heart.

RESPONSIBILITY

Webster's defines *responsibility* as "the quality or state of being responsible.... Moral, legal, or mental accountability....

Reliability, trustworthiness."[4] So what does this mean for young people? "Moral, legal, or mental accountability," as it pertains to responsibility, carries with it an overriding presumption: that kids understand what these terms mean and why they are important. It assumes they have been taught—verbally or by example—what it means to be responsible.

Genetics, income, and ethnicity have little to do with why some children/teens are more responsible than peers or even their siblings. Responsibility develops as a result of parents who provide opportunities for their children to demonstrate age-appropriate behaviors, all the while lovingly holding them accountable for the choices they make. Providing this integrated guidance and support in order to increase the likelihood of their children making responsible choices can be a challenge. The process begins with parents who are unified in how they raise their children.

Unified Parenting

Conflicts are inherently present along the way in parenting. They are exacerbated, however, when parents stand at opposite ends of the parenting continuum. Getting parents on the same page is the first step in fostering responsibility in children. Here's why.

When conflicts arise because of rules—and they will—your kids will exploit your parenting weaknesses. (Oh, yes...they will.) If you and your spouse aren't in agreement on how you will deal with rules and consequences, your kids will usually accomplish their objective: removal of consequences for their actions. If you allow this to happen frequently, you can pretty much forget about promoting responsible behaviors. Talk with your spouse before an infraction occurs to determine the consequences your child will incur when they break your rules.

RESPECT

I purposefully procrastinated as I worked on this chapter. It might not be the best approach to take when trying to write a book, but I was trying to sort out how to address the all-encompassing value of respect. This term has been so cavalierly used in recent time that its meaning has become muddled. *Webster's* defines respect in many ways, including "to consider worthy of high regard, to esteem, and to refrain from interfering with."[5] Historically, respect meant holding someone, something, or some event in high regard with the desire to commemorate. Today, even though children are encouraged to respect rules, respect adults, and respect one another, the word *respect* has become so diluted that it has lost its ability to affect change. Therefore, a little clarifying of these phrases is in order.

Respect the Rules

For children to respect rules, they must be given the liberty to test boundaries. A parent's challenge in this regard is that they not regulate every facet of the children's lives, but instead offer age-appropriate boundaries that allow the child to self-determine. What are you doing to help your children respect family rules? Do they know for the most part what it means to respect parents, siblings, friends, toys, or pets?

For example, I had a student in my office who lacked a proper understanding of how to engage with his parents. Interestingly, his mom kept reminding him to be respectful when speaking to her or his dad, but she didn't point out how or what he was saying that was disrespectful. Before the student and I could move forward in our discussion, we had to clarify how we were going to respond to one another. Once the guideline was established, I was able to point out specific instances of disrespect and point him back to our initial discussion about respecting one another.

Respect Adults

To presume kids will respect adults by default is a *big* assumption. Early on, kids seem to "navel gaze" a lot. They do not *consider* other people's feelings, thoughts, or actions, but they do *observe*. They are watching what you do and say and how you act toward others.

An important and healthy way to demonstrate respect to a child occurs when parents seek forgiveness and reconciliation from each another. How we respond emotionally, physically, socially, and intellectually to those who hold differing views also reflects and demonstrates respect (or lack thereof). This places parents, educators, and coaches in a tremendous position of influence.

Parents have been gifted with the privilege of raising young men and women who we hope will one day demonstrate respectful behavior by taking care of their aging parents. If this thought alone doesn't make us stop and take pause, then I am not sure what will.

Respect One Another

Working with students from around the world is part of what makes international education such a wonderful experience. With such diversity, however, come differences. Respecting one another isn't so much about accepting others' views as it is tolerating them.

To tolerate is to have a fair, objective, and permissive attitude toward those whose opinions, practices, ethnicity, religion, and/or nationality differ from one's own. Acceptance, on the other hand, has the connotation of agreeing or embracing the views of another person. We can, and should, tolerate differences respectfully, while at the same time be afforded an opportunity to discuss and debate our own and other worldviews. Each of us has unique life experiences that contribute to our understanding of others and ourselves.

Educating children to respect one another involves—you guessed it—teaching. And the best way to teach this is through example. As adults, we must be conscious of how we interact with others in the community, on the playground, at sporting events, attending concerts, and when discussing political, social, or religious issues. A child's eyes and ears are the windows to their heart. What we teach through our actions regarding respect is an indication of what is in ours.

FAIRNESS

Spend any appreciable amount of time around elementary students, and you know the frequency with which they repeat the mantra: "That's not fair!" Whether during recess or in the classroom, kids this age tend to view fairness in stark contrasts:

classmates who don't share, who cut in line, or who take their snacks. As children mature, their understanding of fairness broadens, and they come to appreciate just how unfair life can be—those who do wrong appear to go unpunished; children get sick and die; people starve while corrupt government officials prosper—the list goes on.

There are several attributes ascribed to fairness, including *just, impartial, unbiased, dispassionate*, and *objective*. According to *Webster's*, fairness implies "an elimination of personal feelings, interests, or prejudice so as to achieve a proper balance of conflicting needs, rights, or demands."[6] Sometimes, fairness requires following a standard, while at other times it may involve less precision. What is fair may not always be what is equal. Fairness has the connotation of both law and proportionality.

Helping children understand the ways of fairness isn't something to be left to the media or to academic institutions. It may be helpful to draw relevant examples of fairness from culture, but unless we have a moral filter already in place to gauge fairness, we do little more than barrage kids with feelings-based values. What this essentially means is the standard for fairness becomes what feels right. The difficulty with this philosophy is that feelings change. And, as we all know, kids' feelings change often.

Throughout much of early childhood (prior to age ten), parents act as a child's primary moral filter. Author H. Jackson Brown encourages parents to "live so that when your children think of fairness, caring, and integrity, they think of you."[7]

What filters are you using to help your children understand fairness? Below are three suggestions for parents to consider as starting points for cultivating fairness in their children's lives.

Take the Initiative in Being Fair

Don't wait for others to be fair before you demonstrate fairness. This principle is embodied in the Golden Rule: "Do unto others as you would have them do unto you." This is a proactive response, one that counteracts the tendency to apply different standards of fairness based on preferential treatment. Sadly, some view fairness as a commodity, believing that "if I demonstrate fairness, then so should others." However, we treat others fairly, not because we demand this in kind, but to demonstrate respect toward our fellow man. When we keep score of who is and who isn't being fair, we place others and ourselves on a competitive, comparative, point-keeping treadmill, choosing to demonstrate fairness only to those who return fairness in kind. Worse still, the competition may lead us to deem that we've been fair enough and now we have the right to act unfairly. This doesn't mean we don't seek justice or we simply take it when others are acting unfairly. Rather, we hold one another account-able, focusing on the infraction and not the feelings.

Be Consistent

Aim for consistency in both word and deed. There should be coherence between what we do and what we say. Our goal as parents should be modeling a consistent practice of demonstrated fairness. For example, when your child violates rules and you follow up with consequences (as I hope you do), are those con-sequences consistently fair? Were the consequences carefully thought out at the time the rules were established, or are you being emotionally reactive when rules are violated? When we respond emotionally to broken rules, we run the risk of being overly punitive, or conversely, we might mitigate the seriousness of a violation. Both actions result in parental authority being undermined. In either case, a sense of fairness is lost. When it comes to rules, consistency translates to being fair.

In school settings, the administration demonstrates fairness by handling similar infractions consistently. For example, at my present school, if students choose to drink during out-of-country, school-sponsored events, even after being told the repercussions ahead of time, the consequences are consistently the same. This is regardless of a student's class rank, social status, athleticism, or artistic ability. To treat students differently on this issue would result in a loss of administrative integrity. Parents may believe the penalty for first-time offenders is severe; however, it's the consistency of expectations that creates an environment of predictability, which contributes significantly to school stabil-ity and student safety.

Teach Kids to Own Up to Their Actions

From an early age, we encourage our children to apologize for hurting another or violating a rule, but how often do we follow up our teaching and modeling by asking *why* the child is sorry? Parents have a responsibility to help their children understand what it means to own up to their actions. It's not unusual when a kid apologizes, but it may not be because they are sorry for committing the infraction. Rather, they are sorry because they got caught! There is a marked difference between these apologies. It's also important for parents to understand the why behind their child's apologies. When they do, they can help kids take ownership of their choices and actions and thus cultivate a richer appreciation of fairness.

COMPASSION

Webster's defines *compassion* as a "sympathetic consciousness of others' distress with a desire to alleviate it."[8] Compassion requires more than empathy (the ability to understand the feelings/emotions of another); it has the added component of alleviating or reducing the suffering of another. Compassion expresses itself both in words and actions and is a central tenet of most world religions.

• In the Jewish tradition, God is described as "merciful and gracious, long-suffering, and abundant in goodness and truth," (merciful and gracious is synonymous with compassion),[9] and is invoked as the Father of Compassion.[10]

• Buddhists follow the adage of the Buddha that says, "Compassion is that which makes the heart of the good move at the pain of others. It crushes and destroys the pain of others; thus, it is called compassion. It is called compassion because it shelters and embraces the distressed."[11]

• In Islam, paramount among Allah's attributes are mercy and compassion. Allah is described as more loving and kind than a mother to her child.[12]

• Christians describe Jesus as the very essence of compassion. His testimony challenges followers to forsake their desires and to act compassionately toward others.[13]

Philosopher Arnold Schopenhauer notes, "Compassion is

the basis of morality."[14] Unfortunately, much of the media's focus these days isn't on compassionate acts but selfish human actions involving hatred, indifference, and tyranny. At times, it appears we live in a world where there's a sense of disorientation resulting in a kind of moral amnesia. We have a notion things aren't as they should be, yet we struggle with knowing what they ought to be.

Being a person of compassion is one way we can make right what appears to be wrong with our world. Sometimes our tendency is to think our compassionate acts should be grandiose, but such is not the case. The smallest deeds committed under the banner of compassion are greater than the grandest of intentions. In fact, it's often those seemingly insignificant acts that weigh most on the scales of humanity.

We must also consider this: In both home and school, kids occasionally act in unbecoming ways that require correction (so too do adults). Suppose, for example, a student is caught cheating on an exam. Those in authority might overlook, rationalize, or justify the infraction, thinking they are being compassionate. They are not. Demonstrating compassion does not mean a child should be absolved from responsibility for their actions. This does nothing to cultivate compassion in the child, either. Rather, it is by walking them through the process of accountability with the intent to restore their dignity, that we model compassion.

FAQs

With so many different cultures and cultural practices, have you noted significant differences in the way people live out these cornerstone character traits? In the past twenty-two years, having worked with students and parents representing hundreds of countries, I've seen wide variation in how character attributes are lived out, but they have little to do with a person's country of passport. Within every culture, there is widespread variation on what it means to embody character attributes. While a culture may have a general sense of what it means to be responsible or to demonstrate fairness, how these character traits are manifested from home to home varies markedly. What I've noted with increasing concern is that parents who minimize values and character traits do it for fear of being viewed as too repressive, too conservative, or too restrictive by their own kids. In doing so, parents unwittingly contribute to raising kids who have no convictions, which leaves them vulnerable and easily swayed.

How do we help our children cultivate an attitude of compassion? It begins by modeling compassion, in both word and deed, toward those closest to you. How you model this virtue with your spouse says volumes to your children about how compassion works. Committing time for family service projects is a good way to demonstrate compassion. Be sure, however, that your kids understand that compassion isn't a once-a-year event; it's a habit of the heart.

How have you seen character working itself out in the day-to-day lives of kids? I'm reminded of a recent school situation in which a student inadvertently misplaced a large sum of money. The student searched frantically for these funds, but could not locate them. She left the money in her locker with her clothes when she changed for physical education class. While she was in class, someone took it upon themselves to liberate this money. Some kid made a conscious choice to take from another simply because they could. They violated her trust.

Parents must remember: character development and maturation is an active, dynamic process. Kids will be tested, pushed, and pulled in many ways. Often, they fail. When they do, we must lovingly help them pick up the pieces, move forward, and learn from the not-so-good choices they've made, all the while encouraging their growth. For character to grow, it must be practiced. Don't worry, parents, life will bring along plenty of opportunities for growth. And sometimes the story will have a happy ending. The culprit who took the young lady's money was apprehended thanks in part to the school's closed-circuit TV. He confessed and returned the funds, and her faith in humanity and justice was restored.

What role should the school play when it comes to teaching character? Schools may play a supporting role in character development. This may take the form of guidance lessons, homeroom, or a program similar to the one we call "advisory." Advisory is where small groups of students meet with a teacher/mentor twice a week during their four years of high school. The same kids, the same mentor, for four years. During this time they talk about life issues—social, moral, political, economic, religious, etc. Nothing is left off the table. No grade, just doing life together. It's a great time to learn and grow. This dedicated time is primarily for helping kids keep good company with one another and to learn additional lessons about character development. Teachers and coaches may also play supporting roles in fostering character. Most of us can recall a certain teacher or coach who spoke life truths into our hearts that made all the difference in our growth and development. My hope is that schools will be just as deliberate when it comes to fostering character development as they are about promoting traditional academics.

The operative words in my reply to this question are *supporting role*. It is hoped that what schools are teaching is an extension of what is being actively taught, modeled, coached, and cultivated *in the home*. Character development originates in the home. It's a process that begins in infancy and carries on throughout the life of a child. It doesn't end at adolescence or graduation. Long after a child leaves the home, they'll continue to look to parents to learn valuable life lessons regarding character. In this respect, our work as parents continues long after our kids leave the nest. Character programs in school settings aren't about achieving a learning goal as much as they are about continuing to cultivate a heart.

4

Fostering an Attitude of Gratitude

*In daily life we must see that it is not
happiness that makes us grateful,
but gratefulness that makes us happy.*

DAVID STEINDL-RAST

Linda didn't know what to expect. This was her first time living outside of Canada, and at age fifteen, it was the first time she'd ever volunteered for anything. Growing up in affluence hadn't prepared her for what she was about to encounter—poverty, homelessness, hunger, and heartache. Part of the reason her parents took an international assignment was to expose her to the painful realities others face. Her parents were first generation out of poverty, and while Linda found the stories of their childhood experiences interesting, she hadn't internalized them. The service trip wasn't an attempt to make her feel guilty; it was intended to foster in Linda an attitude of gratitude.

For the next week, she and her family helped build homes—but not the kind found in her native Toronto. These homes consisted of four cement pillars, six feet off the ground to prevent flooding, with walls and a roof made of tin. The entire structure was little more than 3x3 meters. The families receiving the homes were grateful, offering fruits, wicker crafts, and other small items as tokens of gratitude.

What began as a single service trip ten years ago turned into Linda's career. After finishing her studies at university, she decided that working in developing countries was what she enjoyed most. Interestingly, this was more than her parents had bargained for.

"They encouraged me to reach out to others in need but hadn't anticipated I would turn this into a career. Strangely," Linda continued, "I'm now teaching them about service and gratitude."

&

In addition to teaching kids right from wrong, parents are also responsible for cultivating gratitude. A friend and colleague who raised two grateful kids reminded me of this after a not-so-grateful experience at the park with my children, then four and seven years old. They whined about the long drive, complained about riding bikes in the heat, and sulked when they didn't get a can of soda. Their ungrateful attitudes persisted throughout the entire excursion. By the time we returned home, *I* was grateful they could spend some time alone—in their rooms! To be fair, I owned half the problem. I wasn't doing my part to remind, reinforce, and teach them how to be grateful. I had wrongly assumed being grateful was something that occurs naturally, not something I'd have to instruct, rehearse, and model. My friend's timely advice was a reminder that we had work to do.

In my work with parents, I often use the following baseball analogy to help them understand what it means to cultivate gratitude. Many children are born on third base. They are somewhat delusional, however, because they think they hit a triple to get there. Their estimations of themselves and their abilities, achievements, and accomplishments are such that they believe they have earned their positional status in life. Sometimes, instead of being grateful, they have an attitude of entitlement that, left unchecked, leads to narcissism.

The catch for parents is, if our kids are ungrateful, it may have more to do with what we've been teaching them than with how well they perceive they can swing a bat.

FOUR SUGGESTIONS FOR FOSTERING GRATITUDE

Express It

Gratitude isn't gratitude if it's not expressed in word or deed. In this regard, the smallest word or deed is better than the grandest of intentions. Not even good intentions count. When we assume others know how we feel about them or believe others should do their work out of responsibility but don't express our thankfulness for what they've done, we lack gratitude.

A former coworker recently resigned from a position where he had served with excellence for seventeen years. He was and is among the best of the best at what he does, yet he felt unappreciated and undervalued. With few words of affirmation and even fewer expressions of gratitude from those in leadership, he came to see himself as a cog in the wheel of a large organization. His decision to leave, in large part, was the result of not feeling valued by those charged with overseeing his work.

Gratitude manifests itself through generosity. In other words, gratitude isn't gratitude until it's expressed. Thinking of being grateful toward another and not expressing it is actually a form of ungratefulness. An occasional word of thanks, some verbal recognition, a simple gift commemorating a milestone—these are small but significant investments in the lives of those you live and work with. This relates to family and friends as well as coworkers or employees.

Be Intentional

Gratitude isn't something that develops intrinsically. It must be coached, rehearsed, and put into practice. It may seem inauthentic to say to your child, "What do you say when someone gives you something, lends you a hand, waits for you, collects your dishes, takes you someplace, plays catch, goes for a walk, drives you to and from practice, or opens a door for you?" Initially, gratitude is inauthentic because children mimic behaviors long before they internalize them. When you prompt a thankful response, you are coaching them. Gratitude comes with repetition, rehearsal, and revision. And like a muscle, it must be exercised to grow.

Provide Real Life Examples

Sharing experiences that helped you develop a grateful heart, recounting stories of other grateful people, and providing opportunities to express gratitude are but a few ways parents can provide life examples.

On a practical note, if you have a helper, maid, or hired worker in the home, do your kids see that person as a servant or as a fellow human being with dignity and worth? How you treat those who serve your family will clearly model gratitude (or entitlement) to your children. Domestic helpers play a significant part in many international homes. I know of a family who demonstrated their appreciation for their helper by financing and building a home for her in her native country. For several years, they provided funding for this project and even traveled to her home to help with construction. Their children experienced firsthand what life was like for someone they have a strong affection for, who was perhaps not as privileged as they were. Even after heading off to university, the kids remain in contact with her through social media.

Avoid Keeping Score

When a grateful person realizes what they have, the desire to share often follows. That generosity then breeds more gratitude. Gratitude and generosity should not be a score-keeping sport, however. Broadcasting your own good deeds does not encourage others to respond in grateful ways, but it does expose the giver's prideful heart. Generosity can feel wonderful when others acknowledge it, but recognition should not be the primary motivator behind it.

Gratitude manifests itself in many ways. Some give financially, others give of their time, some use their talents to express it (making a thank-you card or writing a poem), and some use a combination of ways. One isn't better than the others. The question is, what's the attitude of the heart?

FAQs

When we grew up, we were poor by many standards. We worked hard, earned our way through school, and provided for our family. Our children didn't have to endure this. They didn't experience the cost, but they are experiencing the benefits. Without using guilt, how can we help our kids recognize the cost of what we went through and to value hard work, sacrifice, and grit? Parents can guilt kids into just about anything, including service, but gratitude in this form is short-lived. Sadly, the form and flavor many conversations take when speaking of gratitude is guilt (i.e., you should be glad you're not poor; you have food on your plate and a room of your own). Our charge isn't to make our kids feel bad for their lot in life. Rather, it's to help them, in loving caring ways, understand the sacrifices that parents and others have had to make to provide this better life. This is heavy lifting but necessary work. It will require of parents proactive, intentional behaviors focusing on routine. Thanking someone for something they do, saying please and thank you, having responsibilities in the home, and yes, even serving others outside the family—these are ways to foster gratitude. And as I mentioned earlier, sharing stories from your life or others' lives is a wonderful way to illustrate what form gratitude can take.

Sometimes in school settings, kids attend assemblies where a banquet is used to illustrate poverty. The top 1 percent, usually twenty to thirty kids, are given 80 percent of the food, and the remaining 20 percent or less is divided out among the remaining students, typically three hundred or more. Do kids really absorb the lesson here? The illustration that others have more and the rest have less is both educational and a form of indoctrination. The goal is to demonstrate just how few have so much and to raise awareness of the need to redistribute what the top 1, 5, 10, or 20 percent have. Instead of working on raising the standards of *all* people, however, the focus shifts to making the top 20 percent feel guilty for what they have—or worse, to guilt kids into service.

As John F. Kennedy said, "A rising tide lifts *all* boats" (emphasis mine).[1] To assume 1, 5, 10, or 20 percent have much and 80 percent or more don't because the wealthy took it isn't square math. The underlying or overt message is that those at the top have prospered by taking deliberate advantage of those at the bottom.

You can tell I'm not a fan of guilt-based giving. I am, however, a proponent of service and generosity as an expression of gratitude. While the core values of many schools may embody noble character attributes, how these are disseminated and taught will differ markedly from teacher to teacher and school to school.

I sometimes hear colleagues speak of the need for the rich to give more. I often follow up this comment by asking, "As a percentage, who are the wealthy? Those in the top 5, 10, or 20 percent?" I then present figures from the Internal Revenue Service.[2] The average US family earns approximately $56,000 a year. This puts many international teachers in the top 15 to 20 percent of US income earners. The conversation turns as many shake their head in disbelief. Some of the teachers and school staff workers are shocked to hear that they *are* the wealthy.

The notion that those who are rich should give or pay more should begin with our own personal conviction and action; we shouldn't be forced, bribed, or guilted into giving. This kind of giving is neither gratitude nor generosity; nor does it foster either action.

We take a service trip once a year as a family. Do you think this is a good thing for fostering gratitude? Service trips are excellent opportunities for families to demonstrate gratitude. These trips are also powerful ways to bring different people together to serve the needs of those less fortunate; however, they shouldn't be our primary form of expressing gratitude. It's like asking if exercising once a month will get me in shape. A feeling of euphoria or an endorphin rush might occur, but those are short-lived. We need consistent, daily opportunities to express gratitude for it to grow. Again, service trips are great, and I strongly support them, but not as a primary means of teaching or expressing gratitude.

Any suggestions for expressing gratitude more frequently? The most practical place to express gratitude is in the home. Look for ways to demonstrate a thankful heart toward family members. Maybe it's thanking your spouse/partner for something they do on a regular basis, or a child for completing a chore without being prompted.

One could argue then that people are just doing what's expected of them, and we needn't thank them simply for fulfilling their role as a member of the family. I wouldn't argue with this assertion, but I've found saying "thank you" goes a long way in communicating your feelings with those closest to you. Recognition of an act of service, even those that seem mundane, will always be appreciated. When was the last time you took a few moments to thank your partner, specifically and genuinely, for the things they do to support you, the kids, and the family? Try it and see what happens. Authenticity and gratitude are great foundations for any relationship.

5

Questioning Faith

The important thing is not to stop questioning. Curiosity has its own reason for existing. One cannot help but be in awe when [contemplating] the mysteries of eternity, of life, of the marvelous structure of reality. It is enough if one tried merely to comprehend a little of this mystery every day. Never lose a holy curiosity.

ALBERT EINSTEIN

Fifteen-year-old Dale slouched on my office couch as his parents pressed him for understanding. "Why would you do it? How could you do this? Why would you take other kids' money and phones?" His mom's rapid-fire questions left little room for Dale to reply.

"What do you want from me!" Dale snapped. "You control everything in my life. I have to go home at a certain time, study at a certain time, go to bed at a certain time, and go to church twice a week. I can't choose anything!"

"You chose to steal, didn't you?" I interjected.

My question was left unanswered as Mom proceeded with her interrogation. "This isn't what we've taught you, nor what we believe God teaches. That's the problem."

Dale shot back, "This is all about what *you* believe. What about what *I* believe? I don't give a damn about your faith, your God, or your church!"

❧

Overseas communities form pluralistic cultures. Our journeys abroad not only expose us to various cultures but also to differing religious and spiritual practices. Ultimately, it's from the outworking of one's faith or beliefs that character attributes

45

and values are derived. Sometimes our tendency is to relegate faith to a geographic location, but it can't be so easily compartmentalized. Expected or not, living abroad will bring a greater understanding and appreciation of faith, both within and across cultures. For the record, I would include atheism and agnosticism in this discussion, as both are forms of faith and both shape morals and values.

Readers may object to a school psychologist writing on the topic of faith, noting that this should be left for parents to discuss with their children in the home. I couldn't agree more. My purpose in writing this is to encourage parents to have conversations with their children regarding faith, values, and beliefs. Sadly, some parents abdicate this most important of responsibilities, delegating it to educators. Others extract the essential meaning of faith to "Do unto others as you would have them do unto you." While this is a powerful message, it does little to answer the deeper questions of life, namely those of origin, meaning, morality, and destiny. How these four concepts are understood shapes much of our worldview, and parents are the first in a series of adults that kids will look to for understanding.

Origin
Where did we come from? Each faith has differing answers. For example, Hinduism teaches the universe undergoes cycles of creation, preservation, and dissolution. Islam and Christianity hold to the idea of a monotheistic God who created the universe. Atheistic evolution holds that life came from non-life, evolving over the course of millions and millions of years. Each perspective lays a foundation upon which the remaining three questions are built.

Meaning
What is the purpose or meaning of life? Why are we here? Meaning is so vitally important because it gives purpose and direction to one's life. Think of meaning as a road map, pointing a person in a specific direction toward a particular destination. For instance, Christians are taught to love and serve others by following Christ's example of unconditional love and sacrificial service. Doing so helps give meaning to and for the work they do.

Morality

How do we determine what's right and what's wrong? Is morality based on culture, emotions, feelings, or some combination of these? Often, morality includes adherence to a certain set of standards outside of oneself. These may include expectations in the home, the laws of one's country, or religious practices. Throughout history, many cultures and world religions have held fast to their codes of morality. In recent generations, however, we have seen standards both loosen and tighten. This may bewilder young minds when one person behaves one way and another person expressing the same belief behaves another. Being more diverse than the average populace, the international community may cultivate even more confusion.

Destiny

What happens when we die? Does life just fade to black? Are we reincarnated to a higher or lower form based on how we've lived our lives? Or do we stand in final judgment before a god or gods? Beginning with the end in mind, destiny provides purpose and direction for living in this life. In many faiths, pain, suffering, and heartache only have meaning in the context of destiny.

Each of these concepts—origin, meaning, morality, and destiny—must also be sustained in three domains: *logical consistency, empirical adequacy,* and *experiential relevance.* For example, when a person declares, "There is no God" (origin), they should be able to support this assertion logically, empirically, and experientially. The goal isn't to prove but to build a case beyond *I feel, I think, I believe,* which are merely starting points. Rational reasoning (logical consistency/empirical adequacy) ought to be provided as well. Without this, our values and beliefs are primarily driven by emotion, which might explain some of the discord we are witnessing in culture, media, and politics.

The first goal for parents is to self-reflect. Ask yourself how you came to hold the beliefs you embrace. In addition, have you wrestled with questions concerning your own faith? Do you question things concerning the faith of others? These differences matter and, at some point, will need to be discussed with kids.

Communicate why you ascribe to certain faiths, beliefs, and values. These conversations aren't one-off formalized discussions. Rather, they occur around the dinner table, during car rides, at bedtime, and so on. There are hundreds of opportunities for kids to understand why you believe what you believe, and this process begins early in your child's life as you live out what you believe in front of them day by day. Think of this as a lifelong conversation, a conversation that will become increasingly rich and meaningful throughout the years of parenting.

FAQs

What do I do when my child/teen comes home and declares, "I don't believe what you believe, nor am I interested in going to church, mosque, or the temple any longer"? First, when any statement of such import is declared, I encourage parents to listen. Try to understand specifically what your child finds objectionable. Most likely, their objections will fall under the headings of hypocrisy, moral objection, exclusivism, and lack of clear application to life.

While kids sometimes behave in objectionable ways, they do raise valid questions that deserve answers. Be honest about what questions you have had when it comes to your faith; stop pretending you have all the answers! Most importantly, don't panic. Find others in the community with whom your kids might be able to have discussions regarding faith—people who support your worldview or who might be able to help your child process, without conflict, what it is they believe. Actively listen. Ask how this belief emerged and what thought process brought them to this point.

I had a conversation with a father some years ago regarding his sixteen-year-old son (grade eleven). His boy had decided all Christians, beginning with his father, were hypocrites, and he wanted nothing more to do with church. His dad had decided attending church was a principal issue, so much so he was willing to have conflict with his son to ensure he continued attending services. For some families, this may be the way it will have to be. If this describes your situation and you and your child are at an impasse, reach out for help from leaders in your religious organization. They may be able to provide additional support and guidance.

While it isn't the norm for kids to rebel or reject parental faith, it is normal for them to question it for themselves. When given few answers, they will wander away. Mom and Dad, the question for you is, what do you believe and why do you believe it? Have you communicated this with your kids? If not, this may explain some of the angst.

Note: If you are a parent of a teen, be prepared for questions and objections. Know what you believe and why you believe it and be ready to articulate it.

"My kids are teenagers now; they need to figure out their beliefs on their own." How would you respond to this statement?
I've heard this response many times from parents who've given up on discussing issues of faith with their child. Adolescence is a time of increased need for parental support (via listening and guiding), not less. Kids ask questions, not necessarily because they are rejecting parental faith; rather, they are trying to create their own framework for understanding. They need your guidance to do this. Whether you are a person of devout faith or embrace aspects of several, prepare for questions to be asked. Kids who grow up internationally are exposed to several religions, sometimes simultaneously. As such, they will have questions. At minimum, you owe it to your children to help them understand what you believe and how you've arrived at your decision.

Schools do a good job of helping kids understand various faiths, correct? When a parent asks me if they can depend on a school to help their kids understand faith, my answer is a resounding no! In school settings, children are taught, primarily, content knowledge of world religions (the pillars of Islam; who Moses was; where Buddha was born), but little beyond this. Part of the reason for this is that academic institutions have become politically charged. Some teachers fear reprisal from parents complaining that they are teaching children to question their family beliefs. I've met with several teachers over the years who've confirmed this.

Suppose that, in the process of learning critical thinking skills, including the sequence of questioning world views, a student asked a teacher after class to talk about how she could approach her parents regarding her sexual orientation, knowing it was something her parents opposed on moral and religious grounds. What should the teacher do? Some educators believe they will be accused of indoctrination. Of all institutions, schools ought to be the place where ideas can be exchanged and debated respectfully, not suppressed. By no means does this have to fall under the guise of indoctrination insofar as parents and educators equip kids with critical thinking tools and skills to investigate all faiths.

My child is only interested in stating objections to my faith. He has the cognitive capacity to think at deeper levels, but how do I teach him to do this in a way that is critical and not cynical? To help your child think and converse at deeper levels, I would encourage you to help them understand what it means to be a critical thinker. Namely, teach them to seek understanding rather than cast aspersions on the issue. For every question kids ask, they should attempt answering it for themselves. In other words, can they think of a valid answer for the question they just asked? They too have a reference point they use to make judgments. Being open-minded isn't a critical thinking skill. No one is neutral when it comes to values and beliefs—no one. Each of us has a reference point for determining the truth of a proposition. What criteria will your kids use to determine the *truth* of what you're stating when you answer their questions on faith, morals, or values? This is the work you must undertake to move your kids from cynical to critical thinkers.

When it comes to faith, does it really matter what my child believes if they are passionate and sincere? Sometimes kids— and sadly, adults—assume that sincerity and devotion are all that matters when it comes to belief, values, and faith. But this thinking has led, historically and presently, to some atrocious actions on the part of individuals and groups. Helping kids understand that faith, values, and morals are more than a series of "I feel..." statements is critical. Helping them understand the logical consistencies, empirical supports, and experiential relevance of both your and their beliefs is essential. Such thinking goes well beyond passion and sincerity.

Let me also add that those who espouse having no faith still have a responsibility to help their children understand the *why* behind what it is they don't believe. I have found through many conversations with those who have rejected a particular belief or value system, that their rejection is not based on fact or study. More often, they are rejecting the system because an influential person or group of people (usually parents or religious leaders) has violated them in some way. They respond emotionally to reject the influence of that individual, subset, or group in their lives. They go no further into investigating whether the tenets of the belief system line up with the hurtful actions or previously held teachings and beliefs

Sincerity and intensity can also be factors affecting the rejection of ideas, beliefs, and practices. I remember teaching a psychology course where students were encouraged to work through opposing views on various cultural topics with the goal of debating them in class. In a few cases where kids had not formulated an adequate understanding of their perspective, they defaulted by declaring their opponent intolerant. This wasn't the case at all, but it provided an easy out and effectively suppressed further dialogue.

Unfortunately, this is what some parents do when teens raise objections to parental beliefs. Instead of clearly thinking through their own propositions and proposals, the parent resorts to suppressing the dialogue by discrediting their child/teen or even calling them intolerant. This reminds me of an excellent quote by Thomas Jefferson: "This institution will be based on the illimitable freedom of the human mind. For here we are not afraid to follow truth wherever it may lead, nor to tolerate any error so long as reason is left free to combat it."[1] So too should be the focus of our parenting.

Where does tolerance fit into this discussion? Tolerance is an excellent topic to discuss with kids. Interestingly, the historical definition of the word was "to put up with error."[2] Today, tolerance has taken on a different connotation; it means to accept another's beliefs as equal to one's own. Authors C. W. Von Bergen and George Collier put it this way:

> In the lexicon of neoclassical tolerance, respecting an individual means accepting, appreciating, and approving their ideals and practices. To disapprove of others' beliefs and behavior is to risk being branded narrow-minded, oppressive, and intolerant. Those who are intolerant are said to be ignorant, divisive, and prejudiced. They are labeled ideologues and hate-mongers—deplorable persons worthy of censure. Those who hold principles and firmly held beliefs are considered legalistic individuals with nonnegotiable doctrinal convictions.[3]

To evaluate or judge another's beliefs in today's world is akin to being bigoted or narrow-minded. However, teaching kids about differing beliefs shouldn't involve disparaging comments or being inconsiderate of cultural practices that are part of those differing faiths. Instead, the focus should be on understanding *how* the tenets of these differing faiths are lived out. Know the *why* behind those beliefs.

With respect to faith, what's your assessment of today's teens?

Teens and young adults have been hoodwinked by academia, the media, and pop culture into believing that all religions essentially espouse the same principles and are only superficially different. In addition, they are being influenced to believe sincerity and emotional fervor are the primary drivers for evaluating beliefs. Some kids can recite academic differences between world religions, but when pressed further, they will note a belief that the differences among faiths are merely cultural. Yet, try making this claim in India, Israel, Indonesia, or Saudi Arabia. You will quickly find that differences are much more than superficial, and they do matter.

I hope and pray that parents take the time to inform and instruct their children, as well as guide and shape the decisions they will be making when it comes to faith, beliefs, and values.

6

Moving beyond Self

I'm not who I think I am,
I'm not who you think I am,
I am who you think I think I am.

Kenny, age 17

Seventeen-year-old Stephanie was visibly distraught. "I don't want to be known as the person who could only get into her safety school!" She went on to describe her past four years of high school, not in terms of learning, growth, and accomplishments, but as a series of failures and disappointments, culminating with being rejected by her first-choice university.

Her overall self-perception and worth were directly tied to what she had accomplished, earned, and achieved. (For the record, she'd earned close to a 4.0 grade point average.) Never mind her consistent effort, positive attitude, disciplined work ethic, and contributing to both the school and community in constructive ways. Her summary statement: "Life's not fair!"

༄

The way we imagine ourselves to appear to others is fundamental in the formation of our identity, but therein lies the basic problem. Kids don't compare themselves to others by viewing their external attributes against another's, but by comparing their internal perceptions of themselves to another's external attributes. Did you get that? Kids look internally and then compare what they find to what they observe externally in others.

To combat this, pop psychology asserts that children need to develop a healthy sense of self. Commonly used terms to describe this include *self-esteem* and *self-image*. However, as long as the mirror of life reflects on *self*, kids will struggle to develop a healthy sense of identity. Why? Read on.

With cognitive abilities still developing, adolescence is a time when young people seriously begin questioning who they are, what they believe, and most importantly why they believe it. Vital to addressing these issues is the need for kids to have a set of external standards by which they can accurately evaluate themselves. Over the course of a child's life, these external standards become internalized and form the foundation of their identity, begging the questions: "What are these standards?" and "What are the filters kids run their thoughts through in determining self-worth?"

As in Stephanie's story, if a person's worth is based on works (classes taken, grades earned, college attended, etc.), then the value they place on themselves will vacillate. Given how much time kids spend at school and the competitive nature it creates (which is not all bad, by the way), this may account for some of the drama in our kids' lives.

Setbacks and disappointments provide opportunities to refine, strengthen, and grow—insofar as kids have healthy skills to self-evaluate. With care, parents can provide important tools for their children, teaching them to pause and reflect upon who they are and helping them determine where they find their worth. What messages do you communicate to your kids? What filters are they using to gauge their worth? Are you imparting morals and values that will help your children to know themselves, to grow to like themselves, and to find satisfaction in being themselves?

Consider Doug, an eighteen-year-old senior. His family had lived in Hong Kong for ten years, but at the end of his freshman year, his father's job required a move to Singapore. Doug had to say goodbye to his home. He describes the past three years in Singapore as "a living hell." He hates it, and thinks only bad things of the school, kids, and country. What keeps him going? Graduating and getting as far away from this country as possible. Even after countless discussions, words of affirmation, and planning, Doug remains pessimistic.

It's one thing to mourn the loss; it's something entirely different to wallow in it. Doug did not allow his parents' positive modeling and teaching to go from his head to his heart. Some-times this happens, and when it does, it is painful for all. Pain, loss, and separation are part of life's journey. Sometimes kids don't develop those necessary skills without adding more heart-ache first. It isn't so much that he is selfish, just immature.

While I am confident Doug will eventually find his place in the world, I am greatly saddened that he has viewed the last three years of his life as a waste of time. Since his worth was, and continues to be, tied up in relationships back in Hong Kong, he could not get past this setback. If he could not be there, he felt little reason to connect here.

Identity development is a process involving pain, struggles, and trials. (Keep in mind: *pain* is a relative term. Teens respond differently to life events than adults do—things an adult might not consider painful are excruciatingly so to them. The parent's job is to not argue; instead, validate their pain, then help them develop a plan to move forward.) In some cases, kids will be directly responsible for the pain they are experiencing, based on their not-so-good choices. However, life does a good job of providing opportunities for character growth that have absolutely nothing to do with poor choices. Hence, *life's not fair.*

All this to say, without your guidance, your kids may spend a lifetime in search of significance. With it, they can learn to work through and overcome these setbacks and, in turn, become healthy adults.

FAQs

How can I keep my children from viewing themselves as by-products of their performance? When it comes to school, kids derive a good deal of worth, for better or worse (in most cases worse), based on grades. High marks are viewed as affirmation of their efforts. If their marks suffer, then regardless of their efforts, they feel less worthy. My emphasis with kids who are in this mindset is not to focus on the product (grade), but rather the process (study efforts). If after speaking with the child's teacher, I find the student is working to the best of his/her ability, turning in work on time, and maintaining a positive attitude, then the grade is simply what it is. I know some parents will balk at this—they'll hire tutors, impose punishments, or cajole, but in the long run, this only leads to futility. If the student is trying and the teacher notes this and/or if the student is getting work in on time and displaying a positive attitude, then no amount of additional pressure is going to produce a better outcome. At this point, I would encourage parents not to give up. Not all kids learn at the same rate, share the same passions, have the same teachers, or are influenced by peers or school culture in the same ways. What's important is that you can see positive growth throughout the school year. The trajectory may differ from child to child, but growth should be evident. Working to the best of their ability, organization, and a positive learning attitude are the essential ingredients in the growth/learning process.

How do we focus on the process of learning without making it seem like all we care about is the product? Having conversations with the teacher is a good starting point for understanding how your child is doing in school. This also allows an objective third party to weigh in on your child's performance. Doing this every four to six weeks is not burdensome for teachers; in fact, it's often welcomed. Teachers want to partner with you in the process of raising healthy kids. Four-to-six-week updates are recommended when dealing with uncertainties of your child's progress. These conversations go well beyond grades. Let me also add, sometimes the most effective conversations are less than five minutes. Go for a give-me-the-facts approach without going into the drama of what's taking place at home.

How can I help my child develop confidence? Confidence is a byproduct of competence. Competence seldom develops without trials that have resulted in failure (gulp). This is a challenging aspect of parenting and teaching. To be sure, parents can work on building their child's confidence in steps.

At some point, regardless of how much coaching and support is provided, kids will fall short. When they do, they are met with a fork-in-the-road opportunity for growth or regression. Knowing what direction in which to encourage can be tough. Maturation, emotions, genetics, and peer groups all influence a child's ability to grow in confidence. Validating their hurt is an important first step, but the second is just as important: developing a plan. After taking the time to give credence to their feelings, work with your child to make a plan of support for the next steps. To start with, what is the plan to handle the heartache? Wallowing over the long haul isn't a good option, nor is it a plan, but a bit of wallowing is okay. Validate their feelings and press on. The next step: What are they prepared to do, given the setback they've confronted?

Sometimes as a part of the schooling experience, parents may require a child to participate in a club, an athletic team, or a musical performance. (Yes, you can require this, Mom and Dad.) This doesn't have to be viewed as something optional; rather, it is part of the schooling experience. If parents place as much emphasis on extracurricular activities as they do academics, kids will often respond affirmatively.

Note: This isn't an open invitation to over schedule your child's life. We're not talking about filling in every free space on his/her calendar, but we do want them to engage with peers beyond the textbooks.

Schools offer an overabundance of activities beyond the classroom. Parents, don't fall for the line, "There's nothing to do!" that kids sometimes employ. Making some extracurricular activities non-optional is a good start toward fostering confidence. And remember, dealing with failure, developing a plan for reworking the situation, and encouraging persistence are essential steps for promoting confidence.

The world's message is, "If kids aren't the best or the top performer, then it's better not to try. Trying and failing is too painful." How would you respond to this statement? Trying and failing is more painful than not trying. It hurts like hell! As I write these words, I've just gone through an interview process for a different position at my present school, and I was rejected. I found out last evening. I haven't had the opportunity to sit down with the interview team to understand their rationale and most likely won't. At the moment, my feelings are raw. I too was reminded of the cost associated with trying and failing. Like many of you, I've had to deal with rejection in one form or another: I was a welfare kid; the only child in a family of five to graduate from high school; I struggled to get into university and worked through my PhD; there are jobs I wanted and didn't get. Yep, I have had my share of rejection, disappointment, and heartache. I am sure you have too. But failing can produce perseverance, and perseverance refines character. How I wish there was another formula, but there isn't. Character develops through adversity.

Most parents wouldn't intentionally desire for their kids to go through heartache. The good and bad news is, the world will bring plenty of opportunities for pain and sorrow. During such times, parents must help kids move forward. Also, kids can find support from coaches, friends, teachers, and extended family. These people provide guidance, an understanding ear, and even allow for a bit of wallowing in self-pity (but not too much). The pain of not being selected for a spot on a team, of not being elected to student counsel, or of being rejected for a prom proposal bring about intense personal reflection. It's healthy to think about the *whys* behind the rejection, but it's not so good to pitch a tent there.

Another interesting facet of adversity and heartache is that they allow us to empathize with others in ways we couldn't if we had not had similar experiences. I was reminded of this by way of a heartbreaking story a colleague shared. She runs a support group for grieving parents who've lost a child due to illness, accident, or injury. She's been doing this now for well over fifteen years. She brings a unique perspective to this work, a perspective I can't offer and, honestly, pray I never will. She has experienced the death of a child. She's cried a million tears; her heart has been pulled apart in ways I can't imagine—but those who have suffered similar loss know. As she meets with grieving parents, she relives a bit of her loss, but she also offers hope. She will never get over the loss of her son, nor should she. But she has gone through the hurt and found hope, and this is what she offers to grieving parents. The heartache experience allows her to be a comfort to those going through similar experiences. Saying, "I know what you are going through" only counts if you have actually gone through it. What life experience can you offer to your kids to help them understand they too will get through what life brings their way? Many of the issues they face, you have already contended with. And if you haven't, another caring adult in their life most likely has and can be a source of encouragement.

I believe I'm a competent educator because of the experiences I encountered during my own childhood and adolescence. I understand some of the heartache, pain, loss, and subsequent character growth. I suspect many of you parents do, too. I'm actually grateful for the life lessons I experienced. Each of us has a personal story to share as a means of offering hope to hurting kids. Don't just rescue kids when opportunities arise for character growth. Be a rock of support, seek out guidance, but allow the process to produce character.

7

The Cost of Comparison

Comparison is the thief of joy.

THEODORE ROOSEVELT

It didn't matter that Steve was a great kid, well-liked, hard working, and compassionate. What mattered was he didn't consider these attributes something to cultivate. Instead, entering tenth grade, Steve's focus was on externals—appearance, athleticism, academic standing, and likability. In each of these measures, he found himself lacking. To compensate for feelings of inadequacy, he began acting out in unbecoming ways. His parents and teachers grew increasingly concerned. So much so, he ended up in my office. Our conversation about external attributes turned inward to one of purpose and life's meaning. Steve had been spending so much of his time trying to prove his worth that he'd forgot where his worth came from.

ঽ▲

Despite our efforts to help kids focus on self-improvement, the tendency remains for them to look outward for inward validation. Case in point, what is the first thing kids do after receiving a grade on an exam, quiz, or project? They look at their peers' scores and rank themselves accordingly. At some level, we all rely on comparison as a means of validation; but unless it's put in proper perspective, comparison becomes a cruel taskmaster. It teaches Heather there will always be someone smarter, prettier, nicer, skinnier, happier, more athletic, more artistic, and healthier than she is. It teaches Daniel there will always be someone stronger, bigger, brighter, faster, and more muscular than he is.

The extremes of comparison can be overwhelming. Some

kids become ensnared by their shortcomings, believing there's no use in pressing on or leveraging possibilities. Sandra Stanley, author of *The Comparison Trap*[1], points out there's no win with this type of comparison. But what if comparisons could be harnessed to promote healthy momentum? Before this could occur, one significant issue must be sorted: Who or what do your kids look to for determining they are okay? In other words, who or what do they compare themselves against to measure their worth? Healthy standards for comparison must be actively taught and modeled. Without this, kids face the world with absurd notions of what being the best or measuring up might mean. Be sure of this: pop culture and social media, for better or worse, are actively feeding a steady stream of what it means to be okay or how to be the best at _____(fill in the blank).

Comparing one's present situation to others can be a catalyst for healthy motivation. Take, for example, father and wheelchair-bound son duo, Dick and Rick Hoyt. Together they compete in athletic events promoting awareness of the physically challenged. Dick pedals, pulls, and pushes Rick through various racecourses. Together they've completed over a thousand races, marathons, duathlons, and triathlons (six of them being Ironman competitions). When I compare my life and the challenges I face with what the Hoyts have accomplished, it reminds me that if I put my mind to something, eventually I, too, can reach the finish line. Comparison in this form becomes both a healthy metric and a motivator. It teaches me to be grateful and to persevere. Such comparisons can spur on additional efforts, change attitudes, and inspire perseverance.

Begin a healthy comparison by reminding your kids that it's not what they have or don't have compared to others; it's what they do with what they have. Sixteen-year-old Kevin came to see me about not being selected for a position in a school-sponsored activity. For three weeks, he had wallowed in self-pity and was beginning to move his heart and head to not-so-good places. This wasn't the end of the world, but it sure felt like it. The ensuing conversation wasn't pleasant, but it was necessary. Kevin needed help retooling his thinking, to develop a plan. Throughout the course of the remaining year, he applied himself, worked toward his goals, and eventually earned (the operative word here) a spot on the team the following year. This was one of those fortunate endings that spurred on further aspirations.

Unfortunately, not all outcomes end favorably. Does this mean kids should give up, give in, and resolve themselves to apathy? May it never be! We encourage perseverance because we hold out the belief there is something better to be had, something better to be gained, all the while acknowledging present realities. Our focus is on growth, potential, and possibilities; however, none of this occurs when kids fixate on what others have relative to what they lack. I like the acronym GRIT—Guts, Resilience, Initiative, Tenacity—it is the character outcome for kids who stay the course.

FOUR SUGGESTIONS FOR PARENTS

1. *Model and actively teach where your own value and worth are derived.* Allow your kids to question the standards you've set for determining your worth. Provide rationale as to how you arrived at these conclusions.

2. *Validate feelings.* This isn't about arguing why they feel the way they do. Rather, it's about acknowledging the hurt in their heart. Without this, there will be little to no forward momentum. I've worked with hundreds of teens with broken hearts. What I know with certainty is that kids need adults who can relate to their pains, hurts, joys, and sorrows.

3. *Acknowledge present realities but focus on future possibilities.* Formulate new plans and press on. If they persist in wallowing, reach out to teachers, coaches, or other mentors who can encourage positive forward momentum as well. In many cases, kids compare their weaknesses to others' strengths instead of focusing on their efforts and attitude. We must help them avoid this reasoning.

4. *Remind them continually of the standards you use as a basis for healthy comparison.* For many kids, worth is tied to performance (academic awards, athletic trophies, artistic acclaim, etc.). This puts them on a treadmill of anxiety, stress, and negative comparison. Encourage them to emphasize the process of their growth, not the final product. It's the process that produces results, and their feelings are part of this process. Remember, this won't be a one-off conversation—it is active and ongoing.

FAQs

My kids constantly compare themselves with each other. Is this normal? What should I do about it? Comparison among siblings is an all too common phenomena. Sometimes referred to as *sibling rivalry*, these comparison contests take many forms: grades, height, speed, singing, athleticism, or just about anything that has a modicum of metric associated with it. Kids are competing to define who they are as individuals. Children may engage in rivalry as a way to set themselves apart, shame others, demonstrate dominance, garner attention, gain affection, or simply because they enjoy competition. Your goal isn't to stifle comparison, but to bring perspective to it. You can help mitigate the stress around sibling rivalry by not playing favorites or comparing (at least openly) what one child can or can't do compared to another. Celebrate what the child can do instead of focusing on limitations. Finally, be fair when meting out discipline.

When conflict occurs because of comparison, as far as it is possible with you, allow the kids to work out their differences. Sometimes kids seem to only argue in a parent's presence. When this occurs and no sibling physical or emotional abuse is involved, I encourage parents to leave the room, send the kids outside, or distance themselves from these arguments. Leave it to them to sort out. Sometimes the goal of rivalry isn't resolution—it's retribution. In such cases, parents should have a one-on-one conversation with the instigator to help him/her develop healthier ways to resolve grievances.

Lastly, to produce positive outcomes, kids will need help understanding how to argue, compare, and deal with sibling conflicts. Comparison in the form of sibling rivalry is a difficult aspect of parenting, but it is also to be expected. It's not an enjoyable area of parenting, but it is oh-so-necessary for parents to take an active role.

My child is an only child. Sibling rivalry isn't a part of their lives. Are they missing out? I grew up in a family with four siblings and am a parent of two kids. In both cases, I can't think of a week that went by without some comparison among siblings. It seems like this is ever present. As kids, we compared ourselves with one another on the most trivial of scales. But if you are a parent of an only child, rest assured there will be ample opportunity for your kid to compare themselves to others. Sometimes this situation can be more difficult as parents aren't in the position to coach both kids on how to treat one another; they can only deal with their own child. If the comparisons with peers at school or other organized activities become problematic, I encourage parents to help their child work through a plan involving win-win strategies. If this does not prove to be successful, parents may have to intervene. The goal isn't to eliminate comparisons as much as it is to put them in perspective.

I'm having difficulty helping my child deal with the reality that they aren't very good at a sport or schooling at this juncture. I know if they apply themselves and stick with it, things will improve, but they want to quit when they see others doing so much better. Any advice? None of us like to see our kids struggle. It is painful. We question our parenting, and like them, we wonder if things will improve. However, without persistence, improvement is impossible. When it comes to skills development, there is a maturation process, but through it all, loving parents will persist, coach, guide, and sometimes bribe, all to keep kids motivated.

There will be periods when kids struggle with comparisons, but I strongly encourage parents to persevere. Require your child to finish out their commitment (e.g., the current season if sports or music). Partner with teachers and coaches to add additional accountability but don't allow your child to quit. Childhood should be a time of exploration. Kids will try on a myriad of roles. Remind them when they join a team, they are making a commitment; stopping halfway through isn't an option, even if they no longer enjoy it. Next year, if they still don't want to be a part of the team, then this can be discussed, but don't allow them to quit during that season. They are part of a team—others are relying on them to persist, hold up their end of the bargain, and stick with it. I've seen many kids who have reluctantly done this only to find it a turning point for the better in their lives. In other words, when they are going through a difficult phase, encourage them to keep going.

Kids who are doing many things may find they don't feel accomplished in any. Think *overscheduled*. Perhaps focusing on one or two activities along with school is better then five or six. They will need your guidance to learn how to maintain a balance.

The parent role should be one of modeling and providing balance. Allow your kids to make age appropriate choices within the context of the entire family routine. Sometimes kids don't understand this and parents need to step in and help find balance. Case in point, our daughter really wanted to do gymnastics. While I would welcome this for her and I suspect she could be a great little gymnast, the time and commitment didn't work with our family schedule. All of us were sad about having to close the door on this for now, but we encouraged her to explore other possibilities that would be a better fit.

Finding balance is a learning process for both parents and kids and therefore a bit of grace is needed from both sides.

8

When Good Enough Is Good Enough

A span of life is nothing. But the man or woman who lives
that span, they are something. They can fill that tiny span
with meaning so its quality is immeasurable,
though its quantity may be insignificant.

CHAIM POTOK

Are you working to the best of your ability as defined by your teachers? Are you turning your work in on time? Do you have a positive attitude regarding how you're dealing with your schooling?

I posed these key questions to Heidi as we discussed the frustration she felt over her parents' continued efforts to see improvement in her math, English, and science grades.

Heidi responded, "Whatever I do isn't good enough for them! I do all three of the things you asked, but my parents demand more, more, more. Now what?"

&

This is a common theme when it comes to kids and learning. Often there is a disconnect between what kids perceive and what parents expect. When left unchecked, hurt and heartache are likely to develop.

After gathering additional information from Heidi's teachers regarding her effort, attitude, and homework completion (teens have been known to confabulate every now and again, so I check), I was in a much better position to offer guidance to Heidi and her parents. True to Heidi's initial comments, she was working to the best of her ability as defined by her teachers. She maintained a positive attitude during class and was turning her work in on time—yet her parents felt she could do more. "Earning mostly Bs and two As is not our idea of working to the best of her ability," her dad stated.

Knowing there would be several other issues Heidi and her parents would need to address in the coming years, I asked why they felt the need to press this matter. She was demonstrating age-appropriate ownership of her schooling and doing the things we (educators) expect kids to be doing as they move toward adulthood.

"Look," I began, turning to address Heidi's parents, "You folks clearly are concerned about your daughter's ability to earn better grades. However, given her course load and extracurricular commitments (varsity sport and a few clubs), you have to ask yourselves if this is a hill you want to die on?"

Her parents looked at me as if I had betrayed their loyalties. "I'm not interested in taking sides here," I continued. "Rather, I'm interested in seeing Heidi leave your home in a few years time as an independent, healthy, and responsible adult. I suspect you feel the same way, correct?"

"We do," they replied.

"Then help me understand—help Heidi understand—how additional consequences and punishments are going to move her in that direction when her teachers have indicated she is working to the best of her ability."

Her parents sat in silence a few moments gathering their thoughts. Heidi, sitting quietly with an adolescent smirk, could've used a kick in the shin; however, I restrained myself.

"What we want is for Heidi to own her schooling, and it doesn't seem like she's taking it seriously," began Mom.

"What do you mean," I inquired.

"She comes home angry, frustrated with her teachers, and tells us she doesn't have time to eat supper together. She stays up all hours of the night because she says she needs to be online doing schoolwork. And then we see her on Facebook and Skype. I just want to pull my hair out!"

Trying to add some levity to the conversation, I remarked, "Why not pull out hers," pointing to Heidi. (She lost her smirk somewhere between her mom's comment and mine.) Turning to Heidi, I asked, "Can you understand why your mom might feel frustrated when stuff like this happens?"

From that point forward, we developed a plan to help Heidi better structure her time at home. This included requiring anything that plugged in or ran on batteries (namely her cell phone and laptop) to be out of her room by 11:00 p.m., Monday through Thursday. We also discussed ways for her to manage her emotional state.

Mom and Dad agreed to allow her teachers to help gauge if she was indeed working consistently and to the best of her ability with a positive attitude. If so, they would let her be. Doing this didn't mean they were taking a hands-off approach or neglecting their role as parents. Instead, they were taking a step back and partnered with others (teachers, coaches, etc.) as they moved her toward adulthood.

Some parents operate under the assumption that their child should be able to perform with high academic marks across all subject areas if they only work harder. Parenting with this philosophy without inquiring of teachers if their child is working to the best of their ability often involves cajoling, bribing, and threatening, and it results in heavy amounts of conflict. Kids feel like they are on a performance treadmill, and parents feel like they must keep up this pace if their child is going to continue to perform well academically. Talk about exhausting! And yet, to change the course after so many years seems unthinkable...until there's a significant breakdown in the home.

Parents must face the challenging task of helping children understand that the quality of what they produce—in this case, grades—is highly correlated to their effort, consistency, and attitude. If these pieces are in place, the grades will be an accurate reflection of their ability. To continue to argue over their performance is a recipe for frustration and futility. This is why I implore parents to be in contact with their child's teachers when questions arise regarding academic performance.

ADVICE FOR SPEAKING WITH YOUR CHILD'S TEACHERS

Remember the Key Questions

Do you believe my child is working to the best of his/her ability? Is he/she turning in their work on time? Do they have a positive attitude while in class?

Take Action

If, after speaking with teachers, you find your child isn't living up to these expectations, *then* implement a process of helping them own their schooling. This may include arranging for them to work with their teacher during breaks or after school, monitoring what they are doing at home and online, or establishing a study space in the home.

Don't Take Action

If the teacher answers affirmatively for all three questions above, I strongly encourage parents to put the issue to rest. If you continue to emphasize product (earning high marks) over process (work, effort, attitude), there will be conflict. I can't overemphasize this enough. This doesn't mean you should take a hands-off approach; rather, shift your focus to other areas of the child's life that may need sorting before they leave the nest.

FAQs

When my kid has a lot of downtime for gaming, movies, and other recreational activities, why not place more of an emphasis on schooling? This certainly is an option; however, given the amount of time kids spend in school, doing homework, participating in extracurricular activities, along with family commitments, will more schooling promote balance? If you know your child is working to the best of their ability, getting their work in, and maintaining a positive attitude, doing more schooling may not be in their best interest. (I'm sure the kids would agree.)

Your kids are growing up overseas. What other possibilities for learning and discovery might be available for them to pursue beyond the textbooks? They have fantastic opportunities around them that few kids—or adults, for that matter—have the chance to experience. Speaking candidly, my goal for my children is that they have an extraordinarily average schooling experience. I say this with confidence, as I'm well aware that schools overseas are often comprised of students who are two or more standards above same-age peer groups in the United States. I want my kids to have a well-rounded international education, which includes many extracurricular activities.

My main concern right now is that my kids earn good marks. My spouse, however, thinks they should be socializing and involved in other activities. Aren't good marks more important than extracurricular activities? The vocation of children and teens primarily revolves around schooling; however, there are other avenues they must also develop as young adults. Not long ago, I met with the parents of a ninth-grade student (age fourteen). Their daughter had been formally diagnosed with an anxiety disorder. The mother proceeded to tell me she frequently speaks to her daughter about the importance of earning all As. If she doesn't, she would most likely only get into a community college. I was left with little doubt as to what was fueling her anxiety. I asked both parents if they believed this philosophy. The father obviously did not agree with it, but felt powerless to interject an alternative.

As their daughter's counselor, I had to speak into this situation and point out its potentially devastating outcome. I respectfully informed them that I could not support this parental position. What I could do, however, was team up with their daughter's teachers to make sure she was working to the best of her ability as defined by the teachers, not her parents. I also shared, with a heart of concern, that if they continued down this performance-or-nothing road, their daughter would have some significant emotional setbacks. Of this I was sure. Unfortunately, this advice seemed to go unheeded.

High marks are not the only things we should want for our kids, but the cultivation of the whole person. The good news is schools provide ample opportunities for kids to expand their interests beyond books. This doesn't have to be to the detriment of academic progress, but it should be with balance. Colleges and universities are not interested in kids who only have a strong academic profile. They are looking for students who can demonstrate a balanced, healthy life.

What are some markers/guides I can use to know when it's time to defer to others for help with my child's academic or organization issues? By the time kids enter fifth grade (ages ten to eleven), parents should be spending considerably less time directly assisting their learning. Preteens/teens may occasionally need help with their studies, but persistent monitoring of school-work is a bad idea. Why? Because then schooling becomes the battleground upon which parents and teens wage war, often result-ing in pain and hurt for both parties. When parents take on the primary responsibility for their teen's schooling by supervising homework or studying alongside their kids, they promote conflict by communicating that the child is not capable of doing the work alone. When conflict is moving toward unhealthy levels, I will recommend parents defer schoolwork issues to someone outside the family (a counselor, study skills specialist, or tutor). Doing so doesn't mean parents have rendered themselves ineffective in sup-porting their child. Rather, they've decided to focus on other as-pects of their parenting relationship. Ten years from now, parents won't remember their teen's grades, and neither will their teen, but both will remember the conflict from those years.

As I type these words, I can already hear the objections: "If I don't take active steps to monitor my teen, they will fail. I am not willing to let that happen." Most educators will encourage a teen who is struggling to self-advocate, to seek out support and take ownership for their learning. Some students do need additional assistance. Schools often offer services including inclusion/pull-out classes, after-school tutoring, and lunchtime or after-school help. Also, teachers usually make themselves available to kids before and after school hours, during breaks, and at lunch.

What are the signs that it's time to seek assistance?
1. Your kids are using emotions—lots of them—to avoid owning their schooling.
2. You're using emotions—lots of them—to persuade them to own their learning.
3. You're exhausted from trying to keep them organized.
4. The primary focus of communication between you and your kids now involves schooling vocabulary (i.e., homework, tests, quizzes).
5. Your kids refuse to allow you access to see what they are doing online while insisting they have hours and hours of work to do.
6. They use their school performance as a bargaining chip to get you to leave them alone.

What specific questions or areas of consideration should I investigate when sorting out effort and ability? Asking your child why they aren't doing well in school is a broad, vague question. It will only elicit a vague I-don't-know response. Instead, make observations and ask specific questions. When completing math homework, for example, do they use their fingers or other aids for counting and calculating, or do they demonstrate automaticity of math facts? Do they make sequential errors when doing multistep calculations? How do they organize their work on paper? Perhaps they need to use graph paper to better keep steps in sequential order.

This same process can be applied to other subject areas as well. In reading/language arts (English), do they use context clues when reading a passage? When checking for comprehension, do they often look back in the passage to locate answers? Are they whole-word readers, or do they phonetically decode words? Do they understand the elements of an essay and how to break one into parts? Are spelling errors primarily at the beginning or ending of words? Asking specific questions and making observations will point you toward possible areas of remediation.

I can't overemphasize the importance of involving your teachers in this process. Every five or six weeks, ask individual teachers for feedback regarding your child's progress. Be specific about what you want to know. Formulate deliberate questions. General questions (how is Sara doing?) will evoke general responses (fine, great, super). Asking specific questions will get you closer to the answers you seek.

Note: Keep cognitive and social-emotional development in mind. Not all kids, despite being in the same age and grade, develop at the same rate. As your child grows, the subjects that cause them difficulty may change. Beyond that, there are scores of social and emotional variables that contribute to academic achievement. Be aware of these elements before you draw conclusions about academic performance. I remember one student who had fallen in love for the first time with a fellow student. When his advances were rebuffed, he was devastated. He could not have cared less about his next period math test, which he did horribly on. Do you remember what that felt like? All things considered, I could relate to his emotional state, but his mom couldn't. She'd forgotten what love (or infatuation) felt like. Part of our counseling session involved trying to evoke an emotional memory of her first time falling in love. Kids are experiencing many of life's emotional firsts. They'll sometimes be overloaded by emotions, and during those peak times, they will care little about their grade point average, projects, or quizzes.

If I don't push my child to do well, how can I be sure they will get into college? When it comes to motivating your kids, you can do so either forcefully or diplomatically. Sometimes force is necessary to motivate, but in most cases, consistent parenting is what counts—and this is hard work. For many kids, college acceptance isn't so much the issue as it is which college or university will they attend. The answer to this question will, in large part, be answered by the choices kids have made up to this point. Are they consistently working to the best of their ability? Are they turning work in on time? Do they have a positive attitude? (Sound familiar? At this point, I hope so.)

The habits of character and consistency will be the defining markers of success in both your parenting and your child's life. Focus on these areas, and college/university will take care of itself. For the record, secondary schools and universities are changing the way students are evaluated. Memorizing and regurgitating information is no longer the measure for learning. Broader skills are necessary, and these changes are unsettling for some parents. The good news is, kids are adapting to these educational challenges by demonstrating growth, positivity, and a willingness to learn.

9

Doing What Feels Right
vs.
Doing What Is Right

*You cannot make yourself feel something
you do not feel, but you can make yourself
do right in spite of your feelings.*

PEARL S. BUCK

Seventeen-year-old Nathan sat shifting in his chair, glancing hesitantly into the eyes of his parents and then toward me before continuing. "I knew I hadn't prepared enough for the exam and thought if I took all the exam packets, then we all would have to take the test again later."

"Let me see if I have this correct." Pressing him further, I said, "You believed that if you sabotaged everyone's exam, then the teacher would be forced to give an entirely new exam to all the kids, including you?"

"Correct," came his reply.

"At any point in this process, did you think what you were doing was wrong?" I inquired.

"I thought about it, but figured as long as I didn't get caught, it was all right."

"So the ends justify the means?" I offered.

"Exactly!"

❧

One of the pleasures of working with adolescents is being able to discuss complex moral and ethical issues. As they mature and their capacity for abstract thinking and reasoning increases, teens begin to examine their beliefs regarding values and morals.

They will also begin to determine why they hold those views—or if they still do.

In addition to my duties as a school psychologist, I have taught a high school psychology course. Students ranged from fifteen to seventeen years old. We discussed social and cognitive development—how we think and process information. We also considered the formation of values and morals. (When I speak of values, I am referring to the rules by which we make decisions regarding right and wrong, good and bad behavior. Morals tend to have broader social implications and address the motivation based on ideas of right and wrong.)

As a starting point, I posed the following questions to students:

Q: *Does truth exist? That is, are there some things in life, regardless of culture, era, religion, or upbringing, that are right or wrong?*
A: The resounding consensus from the students—It depends.

Q: *Is cheating in school morally wrong?*
A: It's wrong, but sometimes it's justified given what's at stake.

Q: *Is underage drinking morally wrong?*
A: Everyone's doing it [which is, by the way, not true], so it's not considered a bad thing, even if it is illegal.

The students considered these and a host of other questions. The positions they took on the questions reflected their morals and values. While they agreed that character traits such as kindness, fairness, respect, and compassion, should be foundational in all people's lives, the embodiment of the traits in each individual varied considerably from student to student.

PARENTAL GUIDANCE SUGGESTED

In educational settings, teaching morals and values is a main component of the learning experience; however, the primary responsibility for instilling these beliefs must lie with the parents. Author Chuck Swindoll notes, "The job of parents is to help children come to know themselves, grow to like themselves, and find satisfaction in being themselves."[1] For this to occur, kids need guidance, your guidance. As the world moves ever closer to a relativistic consensus when it comes to morals and values, it behooves parents to take active steps to model and educate their children regarding what is true, right, wrong, and honorable. Without this, your kids will be adrift with no moral compass.

Some adults believe education is the key to character development; by itself, however, even the best teaching in the world won't address the issue of character. The formal character education programs in schools are designed to complement—not replace—what parents teach in the home. With these thoughts in mind, here are some suggestions for promoting the development of morals and values in our children.

Practice What You Preach

Morals and values are more often caught than taught. One student I recently spoke with commented that her mother habitually talks about the importance of treating others with respect, yet she treats their helper poorly. Parents must model the morals and values they teach through their own interactions with those closest to them (children, parents, helper, etc.) before their kids will believe those ideals are worthy of valuing.

Be Human

Your kids know you make mistakes; you know you make mistakes. In fact, when it comes to parenting, we often learn the most through our mistakes. When you've blown it, admit it. Seek reconciliation, apologize, and move forward. Apologizing not only demonstrates a desire for reconnection, it's also a great opportunity to model how to repair relationships.

Talk with your child about how you wished you had handled the situation and what you'll do differently going forward. I'm reminded of a conversation I had with a parent who reluctantly agreed to try out this principle with her teenage daughter. The next time they were in an argument and Mom was at fault, instead of becoming defensive, Mom admitted she'd crossed the line and apologized. Her daughter, with mouth gaping wide, was speechless. This was a turning point in their relationship.

Take Time; Make Time

Your child's character is largely influenced by the amount and consistency of time you invest in his or her life. One youngster I worked with several years ago drew a picture of his family without his father in it. When asked why his father wasn't included, he commented, "My dad is at work."

If you believe family is important, model this in your priorities. Perhaps you'll need to demonstrate this point by passing up a promotion that would mean additional hours away from the home. Bank accounts and financial portfolios have value, of course. But no asset comes close to the compounded positive influence you invest in your child's life.

Use Everyday Examples

Mass media provides a plethora of opportunities to discuss moral and ethical situations. For example, take the political decisions being contemplated in the news—health care, military spending, or social programs. When discussing these matters with your kids, be as specific as possible. What is it that you particularly support or oppose? How and why have you arrived at these beliefs? Make sure you provide opportunities for your kids to express their views as well, asking them how they arrived at their conclusions, allowing your kids to share their thoughts, beliefs, and perspectives. Help them by filling in the gaps with information they may be missing. They also might need help understanding the rationale people may use (right or wrong) to form the basis of their decisions, including yours.

You may be wondering what happened to Nathan. Because of the seriousness of the infraction, he was suspended from school. This resulted in his college counselor having to inform the universities he applied to. He ended up being rejected from his first choice university and learned a valuable lesson—the ends don't justify the means.

FAQs

What do I do when my words don't match my actions?
Authenticity is an essential aspect of parenting. Kids, especially

teens, have a "full-of-crap meter" that goes off when parents don't practice what they preach. It's not that parents intend to act contrary to what they espouse; it's that they're human and aren't always consistent. When this happens—and it will—go to your kids, humble yourself, and explain why you blew it. Some parents assume this will lower their status or parental authority. Nonsense! Your kid already knows what you did and that it didn't comport with what you've been teaching. By going to them, asking for forgiveness, and starting anew, you will model what it means to be authentic. To be sure, your kids will see you in a different light when you do this.

Parents must understand that asking for forgiveness isn't a sign of weakness. Instead, it shows how to reconcile relationships. It also positively projects that it's okay to own up to your mistakes. Interestingly, parents who use an authoritarian style of parenting, one with no give-and-take (see Chapter 14), often lack this ability, fearing a loss of parental control. The child's compliance happens because they are afraid of punishment, of being shamed in the presence of siblings, or of not being loved. However, when a parent demonstrates humility by seeking forgiveness, they are actually strengthening their base of authority in the home, not detracting from it. The parent has an opportunity to model how to make right a wrong, reconcile a relationship, and forge ahead in love.

My kids are so busy with extracurricular activities. Do you have any suggestions on how to make time in the day-to-day to cultivate the development of morals and values? Kids growing up abroad have a host of options available to enhance their physical, social, and intellectual development. With sports teams, clubs, and fine arts programs, your child could conceivably spend many hours at school, long after classes have concluded. In fact, schools often function as the hub for the community. The central question to contend becomes: How much is enough?

In the process of enriching children's lives, there may be something parents are overlooking, something far more valuable to a child's psychological health—namely, family time. While enrichment programs at school are an excellent amenity to enhance a child's development, family time is vital in developing psychologically healthy kids who appreciate and respect their parents. I know families who make it a priority to have at least one meal a day together. For some, this is breakfast; for others dinner. Establishing a once-a-week game night, movie night, or even a nightly story time are also excellent ways to enhance and cultivate values.

My kids learn life lessons differently from each other. How can I teach morals and values in ways each of them will understand?
Any parent with more than one child can attest that no two kids, despite genetic and environmental similarities, are alike. One of the enjoyable aspects of having multiple children is each of them has his or her unique personality. It's important for parents to understand the differences between each of their children and to adjust their parenting practices accordingly.

There are core principles and values that, regardless of child differences, parents shouldn't compromise. Fairness, respect, patience, kindness, and a host of other desirable attributes should be fostered in children, regardless of personality differences. When it comes to areas related to a child's temperament, levels of sensitivity, and downright stubbornness, however, there can be wide variation. It's paramount for parents to have a keen under-standing of these personality differences. For example, changing one's tone of voice when disciplining may work well with one child, while raising one's voice with another may lead to con-frontation and emotional distancing. If you know and appreciate these differences, you'll be in a much better position to guide and nurture each child's development.

Each child will relate in ways that are unique to them. For some, it's quality time; for others, it's words of affirmation; others may best relate through physical touch, acts of service, or giving of gifts. (See Gary Chapman's, *The Five Love Languages of Children.*)[2] Be a student of your kids to learn how you can support each one's individual social and emotional development.

10

How Heartache Produces Hope

That which doesn't kill us makes us stronger.

FRIEDRICH NIETZSCHE

What Friedrich Nietzsche failed to emphasize is, that which makes us stronger nearly kills us!

I thought of Nietzsche's quote as I sat quietly with Kelly. What had begun as a single tear had given way to a torrent of emotion. "He was the love of my life, and now he's gone!"

Kelly's father had died of a sudden aneurism a few weeks earlier. She wasn't looking for answers, not now. She needed someone to listen, someone to care, someone to share her heartache. I'm grateful I could be that someone. Through the remainder of the year, we met on several occasions to discuss death, life, suffering, meaning, and moving forward.

Sadly, her father's passing wouldn't be the only loss she would endure. Near the end of first semester, both her grandfathers passed away. Kelly will never get over the loss of her father and grandfathers, nor should she, but she will get *through* them.

It's been a little over a year now. Kelly's attending university, slowly creating a new normal. Her recovery will take time, perhaps a lifetime.

ã€

Pain and suffering often enter our lives uninvited and tend to stay longer than desired. What about your kids? What heartaches have they had to endure? Perhaps a serious illness or injury, rejection, frequent moves, not being selected for a certain position at school or sports team, being rejected from their first choice university or, in Kelly's case, the loss of a family member. The heartaches kids experience are real, intense, emotional, and, in some cases, life changing. Kids must be allowed to grieve in order to heal. In fact, grieving is the precursor to healing.

With the above in mind, I would like to comment on the three stages of a crisis response model[1] that have been very useful for me when working with kids as they address grief, loss, and disappointments.

Ensure Safety and Security

As far as it depends on you, ensure your child is in a safe place physically and emotionally. Generally speaking, the home is where kids find refuge. In some cases, however, the home is where the pain, harm, or hurt is occurring. If needed, seek outside mental health guidance to ensure safety and security. This first step is essential before moving on to steps two and three.

Allow for Ventilation and Validation of Their Feelings

When kids react emotionally (shock, anger, disbelief, sorrow, guilt, shame, etc.) a parent's initial tendency may be to challenge the validity of their feelings. Statements like "You shouldn't feel bad because…" or "It seems a bit extreme for you to feel this way…" typically result in kids closing down or becoming more emotional. Why? Because telling someone their feelings aren't valid is like telling them they shouldn't feel at all or they should feel only the way someone else has determined.

Instead, allow them to vent their emotions, then validate them. When you validate another's feelings, you're acknowledging the pain and hurt they are experiencing. Saying, "I'm sorry you are going through…" or "I can see how you feel this way…" acknowledges that you care.

It is important to emphasize here that validating another's feelings doesn't mean you agree with them. Rather, you are acknowledging those feelings exist, that they are intense, and that you are willing to share in the pain.

Several years ago, I worked with a student who was convinced she had a mental health disorder. She was distraught that no one would believe her. I decided to take a different tack. I didn't discount the disorder she perceived she had, nor did I try to mitigate the emotional pain she expressed; instead, I validated it. Initially, she didn't know how to respond. For the first time, someone wasn't challenging her emotional state, and this confused her.

She once told me, "You're the only person who believed me." For many years she had been trying to convince her parents, peers, and others that something was wrong. It wasn't so much that I believed she had a psychological condition as it was that I believed the pain she was experiencing was real. This was the beginning of significant change in her life.

Predict and Prepare

This last step is essential to empowering and promoting change. To get through only steps one and two of this process is to leave a child spinning their wheels. Instead, begin the process by inquiring what steps they might take to address the hurt they are experiencing. These questions are critical as the answers become a road map for recovery. Ask, what do you think will happen going forward? Or, what steps do you think you might take, given how you are feeling? These provide a context for hope. You want your child to believe there is something better beyond the hurt.

If change is going to occur, they must be willing to do something different. The difficulty with step three is ensuring that we, as adults and parents, do our part to provide the structures of safety and support, and then hold them accountable for the plans of action they/we develop. Through it all, remember: even in heartache there is hope.

FAQs

It's sometimes difficult to understand how not getting selected for a sports team or student government or even not being invited to a friend's house could be viewed as trauma. Back in the day, we'd "buck up," take it on the chin, and move on. Why do kids seem more emotionally weak today? Sometimes we use terms like *resilience* or *grit* to describe one who is able to endure difficulties and yet persist. For many kids, these opportunities have to be manufactured in situations and environments markedly different from those we experienced as kids.

For example, when I was a child, we were very poor. We moved several times because we had no money to pay for rent, not to mention food. Experiences like that can either break a kid or be a catalyst for change. I was also fortunate to have some fantastic mentors who entered my life at key stages to provide the support I needed. Character is primarily developed as a result of going through hardships (in various manifestations), being open to learning, and not being allowed to wallow.

More often today, I see parents who rescue their kids from experiencing loss and pain. It's a given at many schools when a coach posts the roster for a sports varsity team, they will schedule follow-up conversations with the parents of the kids not selected. The parents need just as much, if not more, reassurance and support as the kids. This wasn't the way it was when I was a teen. Parents supported kids at home, helped them grieve, and developed a plan to forge ahead. The rescue mentality is a large part of what is happening these days. It's important when pain enters a child's life, that we allow the hurt to promote progress in the development of their character. (I'm not referring here to situations where abuse is occurring.) Overall, this is a difficult question to answer, and there are a lot of variations as to why.

What do I do if my child isn't progressing through the pain and heartache? I remember working with a student whose boyfriend broke up with her. She was devastated. Despite her many attempts at reconciliation, he wanted only to move on. Her response was a rapid downward spiral of depression and an attempted suicide. I'm grateful she wasn't successful. The pain she experienced was intense. She felt as if there was no out, no option, no light.

Her suicide attempt served as a wakeup call for her parents and teachers. We realized we needed to have a plan of support in place to help. Thankfully, she has moved forward and is now taking positive steps to manage her life. Sometimes, however, this isn't the case. Some kids resist change or are unable to make a change. In these situations, it is essential that parents intervene. This may include counseling, therapeutic boarding school, or inpatient treatment.

As I write this, I'm working with a teen who may well need this level of support. He wants to get better, to move forward, to find a better path. While we are still in the early stages of implementing a plan, I'm not so sure he will be able to persist without additional supports. *All* kids want a positive outcome for their lives. Sometimes they simply can't see a better path. This is when parents must be prepared to reach out for help.

There is a cultural term used in Asia (the region of the world where I presently live) that describes how families are to deal with social/emotional issues in the family. It's called *saving face*. It's the idea that problems should not be discussed publicly. Doing so is viewed as a weakness. Culturally, we need to move past these notions if we are going to help our kids. There are no perfect families, because there are no perfect people. Every family, regardless of culture, ethnicity, income, or social status, deals with difficulties at some point. This requires parents to be courageous, to forgo cultural norms, and to seek help.

Kids in the international community experience frequent mobility that to some may result in feelings of isolation, rejection, and depression. For other kids, these experiences are viewed as part of the journey of life. How do kids handle this experience so differently? This is a difficult question to answer succinctly. Some of the answer has to do with temperament. For others, they've developed—often through heartache and persistence—the ability to effectively deal with the challenges they face. Sometimes it's about allowing kids to struggle through difficult experiences without rescuing them. Sometimes it's about sticking to a task when a kid commits to doing something. Sometimes it's about surrounding kids with caring adults who can support them. In short, there isn't a specific set of criteria that will answer this succinctly. Rather, it's a composite of many quality attributes contributing to the development of trust and confidence.

11

Boundaries

You best teach others
about healthy boundaries
by enforcing yours.

BRYANT MCGILL

"My parents don't give me any privacy. Just because they pay the bills, they think they have the right to ransack my room, scrutinize my social media, and edit my schoolwork. I'm sick of it!"

His dad had found some stuff in Eric's personal space that resulted in the loss of his phone for a week—a death sentence for a teen. He showed up at my office, seeking advice on how to create some boundaries between him and his parents.

"Do you have an agreement that states they can or can't enter your bedroom," I inquired.

"No, not really." (They did; however, Eric conveniently left this out during our initial conversation.)

"Then what makes you think they don't have the right to snoop around when they want?"

Eric sat silently for a moment before responding. "They should know. If they expect me to respect their boundaries, they should respect mine."

≈

When our children were younger (now eight and twelve) we established boundaries governing most facets of their lives. Over the years, our boundaries have shifted, reflecting their development and increasing need and/or desire for autonomy. By design, these boundaries will continue to morph until our children leave the nest.

As psychologist John Townsend notes, boundaries function somewhat like the trunk of a tree.[1] The trunk holds the leaves, fruit, and roots together. However, all trees with sturdy trunks started out as weak saplings. They needed to be tied to a stake because they couldn't yet handle their weight. They needed to lean on and be supported by something outside themselves. Then, in time, the trees matured and took over that job for themselves. Parents, we're the stakes in our kids' lives. The boundaries we put in place help our children shoulder responsibility for age-appropriate actions.

Webster's defines a *boundary* as "something that indicates or fixes a limit or extent; a point or limit that indicates where two things become different; an imaginary line that shows where an area ends and another area begins; and a limit that defines acceptable behavior."[2] Boundaries are essential to raising healthy kids. The following are two areas that may be of help as you establish and maintain healthy boundaries with your children.

Personal Space

"Why do bedrooms have doors if not for privacy," quipped Eric. The desire for personal space is so intense, some kids take zany measures to secure it. I once knew a kid who slept in a closet under the steps because this provided him with a door and privacy. He could barely fit his mattress into his personal space and had little room for his clothes, but that didn't matter. There was a door, it was private, and it was his.

In Eric's case, his dad justified entering his room without permission because Eric had violated the rules around how he was to take care of it. These rules included making his bed daily, not leaving dirty dishes or leftover food in the room, putting all clothes in the hamper, and garbage in the rubbish. Eric's parents had agreed to allow personal space (a boundary) by establishing rules to govern this. Eric had initially decided to abide by them; when he chose to violate them, he forfeited the privilege. And he sulked.

Sometimes—just sometimes—parents do cross the line. Instead of knocking and asking permission to enter, parents violate personal space boundaries. If our goal is to raise kids who respect boundaries, then we must do so too. If you suspect something nefarious is going on, then investigate, but I encourage you to stop and think through the decision before casually rejecting the boundary.

School

What teachers expect of students academically, socially, and emotionally is, for the most part, developmentally appropriate. When it comes to learning, parents must help kids understand where Mom and Dad's responsibility to help them learn ends and where their responsibility for learning begins. This doesn't mean parents suddenly abdicate responsibilities. Instead, they gradually shift their focus from helping their kids with homework to teaching emotional regulation, organization, time management, and self-advocacy skills.

Helping kids with emotional regulation ("Given how you're feeling, what could you do to produce a better outcome?"), organization and time management ("Help me understand how you plan to complete your homework and go out with friends Saturday night?"), and advocacy ("What's your plan for speaking with your teacher about your project?") will eventually result in a need for less parental guidance. Why? Kids will begin demonstrating through their actions and behaviors that they are ready for additional freedom.

A GREAT PARTNERSHIP

When boundaries around schooling aren't established or are violated, the result is heartbreaking. I frequently work with teens who frankly had no business undertaking the academic load they or their parents have signed on for. In many cases, this isn't an issue of aptitude, ability, or intelligence; it's about boundaries, balance, and emotional regulation. These kids and parents are overwhelmed by academic and extracurricular activities; they're sleep deprived and highly anxious. This is what I'm trying to help parents mitigate. Establishing and maintaining boundaries is an active process, one that continues throughout the school years.

If you're dealing with boundary issues around schooling, teachers and counselors can help. This begins by having conversations with your child's teachers. Ask them what your child should be able to do independently, how much time they should spend on a given assignment, and what technology they need access to and how much time should be spent there. Also, share the areas you find most difficult when it comes to enforcing boundaries (emotional outbursts, organization issues, lack of follow-through, etc.) When teachers understand how their students handle their emotions around learning, they can use relational leverage by having face-to-face conversations with those students regarding healthy ways to take ownership of both their emotions and actions. One thing I've noticed with kids, however: they can behave in markedly different ways between home and school.

That's where parent/teacher partnerships can be extremely beneficial. Teachers can help clarify just how much work needs to be done versus a kid saying they have hours and hours of work. In many cases, kids pit teacher and parents against each other, yet neither party has (or takes) the opportunity to clarify what is going on. When parents and teachers do communicate, clarity is brought to situations quite quickly—and kids no longer have plausible excuses. You would be amazed how quickly kids can turn things around when parents and teachers compare notes. This is why I am a *big* advocate for parent/teacher partnerships.

FAQs

What's the difference between a boundary and a rule? Rules are typically directed outward. They often have a negative connotation. Rules are also specific, describing an action or behavior that should stay within stated limitations. Boundaries, in contrast, are directed inward toward self. They are established as a means of self-preservation. Boundaries are about one's personal property line; they help clarify what one's responsibilities are in the lives of others. Boundaries are usually not as specifically defined as rules are. Interestingly, neither rules nor boundaries operate well without the presence of the other.

What common boundary issues do you deal with in your practice? Parental micromanaging and a lack of clear parental boundaries are two of the more common issues I note among parents. Micromanaging occurs when well-meaning parents who dearly love their kids are unable or unwilling to allow a child to own their own learning and behavior. The lack or marring of boundary lines contributes to anxiety, stress, low output, and a lack of willingness to take risks for both parent and child. Other common boundary issues include alcohol/drug issues, aggressive behaviors, money management, cell phone/social media issues, faith, sexual involvement, and defiance.

All the above are areas where broad boundaries need to be unpacked so healthy boundaries can be maintained. By unpacking boundaries, I mean clarifying them to the whole family by stating them as clear expectations or rules. Statements like "you know this," or "we've covered that," won't suffice. Establishing rules that clarify boundaries will effectively contribute to less stress for both parent and child.

What common negative reactions do kids have toward boundaries, and what can parents do in response? When kids react negatively to boundaries, don't automatically think you haven't set a proper boundary or that the boundary isn't working. Rather, these reactions usually indicate the boundaries *are* working. Kids will test whether their parents will let go of the boundary or if they have the resolve to stay the course.

Establishing new boundaries can take up to twenty weeks of parental consistency, and along the way, kids will react emotionally. These emotional reactions may include anger, temper tantrums, willful forgetfulness, martyrdom, badgering, intimidation, threats, buttering up, and more physical tactics. Kids will try to divide and conquer using any strategy they can think of—not because they are bad kids, but because they are reaching for independence.

If you are in a boundary battle, reach out to your child's teachers, school counselor, coaches, or other mentors for help. Unfortunately, living abroad means you will lack access to extended family and a like-minded community that would uphold the boundaries you've established with your kids, as well as support and encourage them to behave as expected. Gone are the days when Mom and Dad could rely on the neighbors to inform them of any antics they should know about. When living abroad, the immediate family is likely all that is there to uphold your expectations. Building a community around your family is as much about supporting you as it is your children.

What are some key aspects in setting boundaries with kids?

The following illustration helps show what not to do concerning boundaries.

Seventeen-year-old Karen (grade eleven) had given up on attending school—not because she wasn't capable, but because she'd lost the desire to continue. She'd had enough of her parents and her parents had had enough of her—and around and around it went. And then her dad's work required he be away from home for five weeks. He was the only one she would obey. Her mother did little more than raise her voice and cry. So Karen continued to come and go as she pleased. Her parents continued to give her an allowance and allowed her to behave disrespect- fully. The home became an intolerable place to live. The family had no boundaries, no anchors, and little hope in the foreseeable future for change.

Drs. Cloud and Townsend, in their book, *Boundaries*, offer four anchors essential to establishing healthy relationships and avoiding this hopeless estate.[3] First, kids must understand that parents are on their side and love is what motivates their actions. The second essential anchor for forming boundaries is to estab- lish and enforce rules. When it comes to parental expectations, children must understand where and what their boundary lines are. Boundaries should be clearly delineated and include both actions as well as behaviors. Rules must be specific because when a violation occurs—and there will be violations—you must be prepared to follow through with consequences.

Anchor three, kids must be allowed the freedom to make choices. Kids can choose to respect or reject the boundaries. Parents can attempt to force kids to comply with expectations, but when they do, kids are likely to go underground with behaviors. The goal is that kids will make positive choices that will garner additional freedom and that parents will see them being responsible.

Anchor four is reality. Reality is defined as carrying out

consequences should a child violate boundaries. Kids need to experience the consequences of the choices they make. This may come in the form of not being allowed dessert, not going to a show, loss of computer access, a reduction in allowance, or missing a sleepover.

Love, expectations, choices, reality—these are all essential in forming healthy boundaries in the home as well as in the world at large.

12

The Truth of a Lie

You are valuable just because you exist.
Not because of what you do or what you have done,
but simply because you are.

MAX LUCADO

"I'm never gonna get better, am I?" Samatha's words punctured the silence that had invaded my office. "No matter how hard I try, I always come up short of my parents' and teachers' expectations."

Knowing I needed to be confrontational to redirect her thinking, I remarked, "You know, Samatha, for a lie to be effective, it has to be believable."

She assumed a defensive posture, slouching further into the couch. "What are you talking about?"

"I'm talking about the lies you tell yourself and then believe them as if they're true. For example, the voice in your head that says you'll never be good enough, no one will ever like you, or you can't do anything right."

Samatha protested. "But those things are true!"

"How so? How do you know they're true? What filters are you using to determine that your thoughts are based in reality?" She seemed confused by the question, so I tried a different tack. "If I said I weighed eighty pounds (36kg), would you believe me?"

She grinned as she pondered the thought. "No, but you would look funny."

"But I am! Why doesn't anyone believe me?" I argued.

"If you step on a scale, people would know you're lying," she parried.

"But they already know I'm lying, don't they?"

"Yes, but now *you'll* know you're lying."

"So is the external evidence countering or confirming my thoughts?" I asked. Samatha got the point.

Over the next several weeks, we scheduled a series of meetings with parents, teachers, and friends, based on the emerging themes Samatha uncovered in our talks. Themes like "I don't have any friends," "I'll never be good enough for my parents," and "My parents love my brother more than me." These extreme thoughts heavily influenced her emotional state.

Addressing Samatha's misperceptions about herself wasn't easy, but if we had allowed her to continue thinking that way without challenge, her spiral of depression, anxiety, and self-injury would have continued. Having conversations with others forced her to confront the perceptions she held in isolation. Over time, and with consistent parental support, Samatha began taking control of her thoughts, running them through a healthy set of filters, and finding degrees of freedom in areas where her emotions had long held her captive.

❧

Our thoughts have the power we give them. Sadly, Samatha's story is a common one. Many instances of anxiety and depression are rooted in persistent and pervasive negative thinking. It's not that kids don't want to change; many simply don't know how. When this occurs, a parent's tendency is either to become manic—running from one emotional episode to the next, trying to assuage their kid's feelings—or they dismiss the behavior as immature and childish. I would like to suggest a middle path—one of consolation, clarification, and confrontation.

When kids (or adults) apply words such as *always, never, all the time, no one, everyone,* or *everybody* to their situations, they are thinking in emotional extremes. If they are allowed to persist with these thoughts, negative, nonproductive patterns will emerge. For example, if your child says, "I can't do anything right," or "I'll never be good enough," they are trying to convince themselves—and you—that they are the victim of circumstances beyond their control. When they adopt this mentality, they eventually take on the role of martyr or victim. It's from this emotional vantage point that they'll justify passivity.

Kids are primarily emotional thinkers. Not yet able to compartmentalize their feelings, their moods color all areas of their lives. Parents must help them sort through their pain, to use words to communicate, not emotions, and to develop a plan of action. With practice and consistency, parents can move kids from being emotionally passive to logical thinkers who can own their emotions. The steps in this process are outlined below.

Consolation—Validate the Hurt

The way to a kid's head is through the heart. When kids speak in emotional extremes, it's vital for parents to acknowledge and validate their feelings. This doesn't mean you agree with the sentiments. Saying, "I'm sorry this is happening" or "I can see how you would feel this way when..." are ways to validate feelings. When you do this, expect them to initially be more emotional. Why? You're providing an outlet for their feelings. Doing this also allows you access to the cerebral side of their brains. In short, they need to be allowed to vent.

Clarification—Ask Difficult Questions

The process of validating feelings and clarifying the issues takes time, sometimes a lot. In fact, your timing of questions is more important than your words. The clarification process is where parents usually run into trouble. Some approach this like a lawyer interrogating a client instead of a parent cultivating a heart. When parents demand evidence to support emotions, the process shuts down. Instead, get your kids talking by asking them questions such as, "When you say you can't do anything right, can you help me understand what you mean?" or "When you say you have no friends or your teachers don't like you, can you help me understand what you mean?" These open-ended questions provide insights into what they are thinking. In most cases, the extremes won't be sustained beyond one or two specific events.

Confrontation—Address the Extremes

Once you understand what the specific issues are, it's time to develop a plan of action. Continued passivity and emotional extremes won't produce positive outcomes. If your child doesn't want to move forward, you must take the lead. Expect your child to either become more emotional or refuse to engage. Have the courage to look beyond the present emotional state of your child and think about how they would like you to handle similar situations in the future. For example, what would you do if your child came to you in tears, stating, "My teacher doesn't like me!" What if they then used this as justification for not putting effort into the class?

After you've validated their feelings and asked for specific examples, it may be appropriate to arrange a conversation between your child and their teacher to clarify misunderstandings. Your child's counselor can work as a mediator to facilitate this process. It's difficult for kids and/or teachers to persist with negative or extreme thinking when a third-party mediator presents the situation from all sides and clarifies any contradicting information. The goal is for kids to self-advocate, address the specific issues and concerns, and seek a positive resolution. This is the kind of work I undertake on a regular basis, and it often leads to positive outcomes.

But what do you do when a child's feelings are accurate? In some cases, kids may not have many friends, they may not be able to do certain things as well as others, or they may be dealing with a personality clash with a teacher. To deny this is to deny reality. Sometimes reality is painful. There aren't quick fixes or easy solutions to some of life's problems, but there is hope. It's important to focus on what kids can do. Can they persist despite obstacles? Can they, with support, find ways to demonstrate competence in other areas?

With maturation, motivation, and yes, emotions, kids can find ways to overcome challenges. A time for wallowing may be necessary, but it's not the place to camp. Sometimes, to get over painful circumstances, we have to go through them—even kids. There's no joy in this, at least not in the immediate, but there are opportunities for growth.

If your child is persistently thinking in negative patterns and you need help, reach out to their counselor or teachers. Kids will need guidance from parents to cope with their emotions, deal with negative self-talk, and find positive ways to own their emotions and resulting behaviors.

FAQs

Can you tell me a bit more about the timing of clarification questions with kids? Because kids are primarily emotional thinkers, the approach we take with them must be timed wisely. Is there a time of day they are more receptive to thinking about what you're saying? Keep in mind the clarification process may not be the time to confront their thinking—or maybe it will be. Here's the thing: When it comes to children or teens, there are patterns of behaviors they all have in common, but each kid is unique in how and when they manifest them. Knowing your child's emotional ups and downs is extremely helpful in having these conversations.

I'm a morning person. I love mornings. I'm up before the city wakes, reading a paper and sipping tea at a local hawker stand (coffee/tea shop). This is my idea of a great way to start the day. I'm most receptive to conversations of a critical nature during this time. Later in the day, I have too many things happening, I can't focus as well, and I tend to be less open to dialogue, particularly dialogue leading to confrontation. Your kids will also have a time of the day they are more receptive to dialogue. It is to your advantage to figure out when this is.

When you speak of passivity, what do you mean? To illustrate what I mean by passivity, I'll share an experience I had with Rick, a seventeen-year-old twelfth grader, who was struggling with friendships. He had made the conscious decision to no longer hang out with a group of boys who were drinking alcohol. This resulted in his being rejected by his peers, which made him feel alone and lost. He began spending considerable time talking about the glory days when he attended a different international school where the kids were more accepting of each other's differences. That was two years ago.

Since then, he has been dealing with fitting in, feeling good about himself, and finding his place at school. Sadly, he has taken on what I would describe as the Eeyore Syndrome. You may remember Eeyore from A.A. Milne's *Winnie-the-Pooh*. His character personifies a "woe is me" mindset, where much of life is viewed as oppressive. Nothing goes his way, and he can do nothing to change it. Sadly, many teens I work with suffer from this malady.

What is most concerning isn't that Rick feels out of sync, but that he has somehow gotten it into his mind that there is nothing he can do to change his situation. My main concern in Rick's situation was to help him take back ownership of his choices and corresponding feelings, and require him to step up and take ownership of his life. This is a challenge for many teens. As long as they allow themselves—or others allow them—to be victims of their choices or circumstances, they can justify passivity and the resulting outcomes. Parents, educators, counselors, and other caring adults must help kids fight against this thinking.

To be fair, some kids experience life issues that are truly distressing and traumatic. These kids do require extra support. In most cases, however, this is not the issue. Kids need validation for what they are feeling, but they also need to move beyond that point, even if they don't want to, to develop action plans that take back the ownership of their feelings and choices.

Some kids will want to wait until their feelings change before they attempt to move ahead. Don't accept this reasoning. Encourage them to make different choices, knowing that their feelings will catch up. Sometimes parents, coaches, teachers, or mentors will need to drag a kid along, requiring them to do something different until their feelings catch up with their new actions.

Passivity is a poison that destroys a child's ability to plan and move ahead. Validate their feelings, allow a bit of time for them to process, then formulate a plan to move ahead.

Why do things get worse when I confront my child? Things get worse before they get better because kids (and adults) prefer routine. Even dysfunctional routine has a measure of predictability. Sometimes the challenge I face when families arrive in my office is simply to de-escalate the situation from crisis back to dysfunction.

Changing patterns is painful. If you've tried a goal of getting into shape or eating healthy, you may understand what I'm getting at. When confronted, our natural tendency isn't to be receptive but defensive. Kids build walls of plausible deniability; they finger point or become angry and sulk. For these reasons, before you confront your child, I recommend you determine the desired outcome. Then, with the end in mind, I will ask this question: How will you address the inevitable objections, conflicts, and halfhearted attempts your kids will make to comply with your parental requests?

It's normal, as kids try to extricate themselves from parental demands, to experience an escalation of tensions, words, and actions. It's during these times parents are most likely to give in, give up, or reach out for help. I hope what drives a parent's resolve here is the desire to raise healthy, confident kids. If this is the filter they run their parental decisions through, I am convinced—in about 95 percent of the cases—that they will achieve good outcomes. The 5 percent uncertainty has much to do with word choices and the timing of conversations.

13

Fully Developed Frontal Lobes:
A Parental Dilemma

What people did not reason into,
they cannot be reasoned out of.

Frederick W. Evans

An aggravated parent marched into my office, loaded for bear (a colloquial expression used to describe someone ready for battle). His intended mark—me.

"I knew your advice wouldn't work!"

Hastily, I fumbled for a large book, cushion, or anything else that would provide a buffer between Clark's razor-edged tone and my targeted personal space.

"I did what you said, and it didn't work!"

"What do you mean, it didn't work?" *That's right; keep him talking.*

"Just like you advised, I told Sam [his fourteen-year-old son] that anything plugged in or running on batteries had to be out of his room by 10:00 p.m. And we were no longer getting him up for school; he needed to do that on his own."

"How and when did you tell him?" I responded.

"Why does that matter?" Clark retorted.

And that's when it occurred to me: Clark was dealing with a full-blown case of FDFL.

❧

Fully Developed Frontal Lobes (FDFL) is a condition in which healthy, functioning parents attempt to use logic, reason, and common sense to persuade their child to make course corrections in their behavior and attitude. Many adults would prefer not to remember those awkward, underdeveloped-frontal-lobe adolescent years. Some even go so far as to deny their frontal lobes were ever underdeveloped. In such instances, only the intervention of an all-too-willing, older family member—typically the adult's parent or grandparent—will be of any help.

Clark and his wife, like so many other caring parents, have plans for Sam. When he graduates, they would like for him to be a healthy, confident, assertive, logical-thinking young man. To this end, they've formulated rules and consequences. The problem: all this makes sense. For his part, Sam too wants to be independent, but he wants this on his own terms and he's willing to use his emotions to achieve it.

When parents fail to account for the lack of FDFL in their teenager, they wrongly assume that if they continue to reason, dialogue, and debate, eventually their teen will come around to their way of thinking. It is true: they eventually will. However, when this doesn't occur on the timeline the parents determine, conflict ensues. Keep in mind that *eventually* is a relative term, completely vague with no regard to time. It could be days, months, or even (sigh) years. The parent's definition is "next week"; the teen's definition is "when I feel like it." It will happen, but don't set your watch to it.

Why the difference in thinking? Physiologically, by age six, the brain is about 95 percent developed, but the gray matter—the thinking part of the brain—is far from fully developed.[1] A mental pruning process that begins around age eleven refines the higher thinking processes commonly associated with adulthood. Dr. Jay Giedd, neuroscientist at the National Institute of Mental Health, notes, "In the teen years, the part of the brain helping organizing, planning, and strategizing is not done being built yet, it's not [that] teens are stupid or incapable of things, but it's sort of unfair to expect them to have adult levels of organizational skills or decision-making before their brain is finished being built."[2] Further, researchers have found that, during adolescence, we rely heavily on our amygdala—the part of the brain primarily responsible for emotions—to weigh decisions.[3]

Knowing the physiology and neuroscience of adolescent brains is half the battle, but what is a parent to do in the interim?

Think Like a Teen without Acting Like One

The primary filter teens use to make sense of their world is emotion. They process their actions and other people's actions emotionally before moving to the logical implications of their behaviors and attitudes. When parents begin discussions with their teens by questioning the reasons behind an action instead of the emotion, parents miss a golden opportunity to learn something about what's motivating their child.

What does this mean practically? The next time your teen does something that results in not-so-good consequences, try asking them to help you understand what they felt when they made the choice or decision in question. Avoid the typical parental cry of "What were you thinking?!"

This shift is subtle but profound. It gets to the heart of the matter. When I ask teens such questions, I'm often met with emotional responses like crying, anger, or prolonged silence. When this occurs, I know I'm moving in the right direction to affect change. The kids are sometimes a little confused as well because they are used to being asked what they were/are thinking. Instead, they are being asked what they were/are feeling.

Validate Emotions

Validating another's feelings ("I'm sorry you feel this way; I can understand why you would be upset when…") in no way implies agreement with them. We validate because we want to get to the heart of the matter, but we must acknowledge the matters of the heart first. A note of caution is in order here: Don't get roped into drawn out emotional diatribes. This will result in something you say becoming the issue instead of something your child did. Many parents struggle with this, believing the time to teach the lesson is when their child is emotional; it's not. Allow for a cooling off period, then come back and address the issue. Also, remember conflicts are often the precursor to change.

Stick to a Plan

Sometimes I work with parents like Clark who are worn out emotionally. They wonder if the infamous battles with their kids are worth it, to which I say a resounding *yes!* No one promised that this parenting gig was going to be easy; that resolutions would present themselves in dramatic movie fashion; or that all matters would work out with kids thinking, "Gee, my parents do care about my best interest"—but we keep on parenting.

Be willing to work through the emotions but keep your focus always on the long-term goals. Your kids are relying on you to see the future and chart the course when the path is unclear. Along the way, be open to input. As they grow and develop, most kids will come to understand parenting isn't all about control, dominance, or power. Rather, parenting is about directing and providing for our children through the preteen years, then listening and guiding them into adulthood. Having a plan is about being intentional.

Don't Be Self-Critical

In a vulnerable moment, Clark asked, "Am I responsible for all this?" (At that point, I breathed a sigh of relief and lowered the cushion I was clutching). According to Clark, there weren't nearly as many problems before the family moved to Singapore. The kids were well adjusted and life was predictable and relatively stable. Now, problems seemed to be the norm.

To be sure, there are some issues that we as parents need to own. We don't always get it right. We make mistakes; we regret doing or saying things. In such moments, healthy reflection can be a good thing. However, when guilt becomes the driving motivator instead of love, homes become places where no one wants to spend time. Mom and Dad, when you're in the wrong, own up to it, but continue with the goals you've set out for the kids.

FAQs

Sometimes being a parent is so maddening! There are times I have to say the same thing over and over, with increasing emotional intensity, before my son will respond. Is there something wrong with him or me? The issue isn't you, at least not initially; it's your child. They know what you're asking or telling them to do, but they also know if they persist in not responding or if they respond emotionally, eventually you'll either give up or give in. The issue isn't your attitude; it's theirs.

If this is increasingly becoming the case, I encourage you to sit down with your child and point out *specific* examples of them not complying with what you've asked. Then point out the *specific* consequences of what will happen if they continue to behave that way. Going forward, they will know what will happen should they persist. The key then is the follow-through. You must do what you've said you are going to do. If you don't, the issue is no longer your child's; it's your parenting.

Our son will argue about cleaning up his room, taking a shower, picking up his toys—anything. He has all the makings of a marvelous lawyer. He attempts to absolve himself of his responsibilities by immediately asking us why. He knows what we are asking, and he knows the reason behind the request. He isn't asking for clarification; he's asking for confrontation. He's looking for an out so he can do what he wants. (Think non-FDFL.) He wants out now; he wants his way.

We had to put a stop to this. Using the technique I described above, we explained to him what we thought he was doing and what we intended to do going forward to put a stop to his actions. Now when we ask him to do something and he immediately throws out the why response, he loses his computer (iPad) privileges on one of his two weekend days. It didn't take long for him to realize it was no longer advantageous to ask why at that moment. His duty is to do what we ask. Once the task is finished, if he wants to ask why we asked him to do it, we're willing to discuss that…but that rarely happens.

Sometimes the only thing kids understand is that whatever it is they find the most enjoyment in—in this case, the iPad—can and will be used against them if they choose not to do what their parents have asked.

Is it unrealistic for kids to learn tasks or different behaviors when the neurological evidence indicates they lack the capacity to fully understand their actions? No, it's not unrealistic to ask young minds to learn before they fully understand. When my daughter was four years old, despite parental warnings, she got too close to the stove and burned her finger. She quickly realized the cost of not obeying. In this case, physical pain was her teacher.

From an early age, kids mimic the behaviors of adults.

While they may not understand the reason behind a behavior or action, they can still perform the task. As they grow, they'll come to understand the deeper meaning behind the actions—this will keep you from harm; you're part of the family so this is why we want you to do this; there is a cost associated with this beyond the monetary, and so on. Keep the focus on the expectations (their behavior) and the consequences (the catalyst to change their behavior). As your child progresses through their youth, there will be opportunities for discovery, conversation, and self-reflection. Sometimes, quite honestly, waiting for this to occur can be maddening. It tries a parent's resolve. The mantra, "Because I said so," can be a useful technique for dealing with short-term frustration, but not necessarily the long-term desired change.

Is there any way to speed up the process of developing healthy functioning frontal lobes? Yes, you can speed up this developmental process—sort of. Physiologically and neurologically, not much can be done to hasten the process of deeper holistic thinking, but you can establish patterns of behavior that may quicken positive outcomes. These include creating routines and consequences that will allow kids to come to own their actions and emotions. It's important to emphasize, however, that even with highly structured routines, kids will sometimes flounder. This is why consistency and predictability must be a part of your home and life routines.

Why are some kids more adept at thinking their choices through, while others struggle to do so? Anyone with more than two kids will recognize this issue. Some kids are born with a greater capacity to deal with adversity, while others struggle. Some kids are inclined to be organized and self-motivated with seemingly little guidance. Others need much by way of direct instruction and counseling. Regardless, kids still need their parents to train them up. Some kids are more receptive to this, but in either case, kids can learn new behaviors, ways of thinking, and ways of owning their choices. Often, it's a parent's tone, tack, and timing that influences the outcome the most.

14

Fostering Responsibility and Independence in Children and Teens

*The greatest gifts you can give your children
are the roots of responsibility and
the wings of independence.*

DENIS WAITLEY

"I'm going out of my mind! I can't make sense of anything Bret's doing. He's throwing his future away!"

Bret's mother abruptly took an unpleasant detour into the recesses of her heart, and what was there apparently needed to come out. "We've provided everything for him, and this is the way he treats us?"

The previous weekend, Bret had hosted a pay-party (a party where alcohol is served for a fee to high school students, who are, of course, underage) while his parents were out of the country. In desperation, they hauled Bret into my office (which I've affectionately dubbed the weeping chamber), hoping I could shed some light on his choices. And so we began.

❧

Caring for and raising kids is one of the most rewarding—and demanding—endeavors adults undertake. The parenting techniques employed during the early years tend to have a compounding effect. Think back for a moment to your childhood experiences. How would you describe your parents' parenting styles? Responses to this question tend to fall within three general, but extensive, categories—*permissive, authoritarian,* and *authoritative* parenting.

Permissive

Permissive parents typically avoid confrontations with their children, don't address inappropriate behaviors, and tend to not place age-appropriate demands and expectations on their kids. Some parents in this category compensate for their child's short-comings by taking on many of the roles the child should be handling (doing their homework, cleaning their rooms, etc.). Kids raised with this model of parenting tend not to take responsibility for themselves or the choices they make later in life. Why? Because either they have been taught that what they do isn't of value or because they have not been held to any standards at all. Further, these kids tend to struggle with both confidence and competence.

Permissive-indulgent parents tend to do too much for their children when it comes to schooling, for example, finishing projects, writing papers, coloring in artwork, completing their third-grader's science projects, and so on. The message the child receives is "what you produce isn't good enough," or "you don't possess enough competence to do schooling." For such parents, much of their own worth and value is tied to how well their child performs. Talk about pressure! These are the kids I see in my office struggling with worth, meaning, and value.

Authoritarian

On the other end of the continuum are authoritarian parents. These parents tend to not allow a great deal of verbal give-and-take. "It's my way or the highway!" or "if I wanted your opinion, I would have asked you for it," might be familiar slogans in such homes. Authoritarian parents can be demanding and directive, highly intrusive, and at times, overly involved in kids' lives. Children from these homes tend to have a works-based relationship with their parents. The child's perception of Mom and/or Dad's love for them is contingent on how well they do academically, musically, athletically, and so on. This is similar to permissive parents, in that value and worth are derived from accomplishments. The difference is, the permissive parents are doing the work, not the child.

Kids from authoritarian homes tend to go underground with their behaviors, living a double life. These kids have two

Facebook accounts, not one. Since they often can't meet their parents' unreasonable expectations, they resort to hiding their grades, dates, friends, accomplishments, and more. When parents find out, infighting results. Distrust, miscommunication, and conflict are hallmarks of authoritarian homes.

I once worked with a naval commander and his sixteen-year-old daughter (grade eleven) who decided she had had enough of her dad's military command style of parenting. She proceeded to dress him down with a series of four-letter words strong enough to make her dad blush. Slouched over in my office chair, he commented, "I am a commander and can tell sailors to come and go, and they obey. My daughter, she couldn't give a sh**." This father hadn't realized how his parenting style was contributing to the problems he was dealing with. Sometimes the first step in affecting change begins with parents understanding and accepting their contribution to the conflict.

Authoritative

The last general parenting style is authoritative, which tends to have a democratic approach with boundaries. A good deal of verbal give-and-take occurs between children and parents regarding rules and consequences, but the proverbial "buck stops here" with the parents. Authoritative parents are proactive and purposeful in parenting but not overly intrusive or demanding. Kids raised in such homes tend to be assertive, confident in their abilities, and willing to take age-appropriate academic and social risks.

When I meet with authoritative parents—yes, they do exist—I often find they have very few rules governing their children's behaviors. Why? Because their children have learned over the years that Mom and Dad will hold them accountable to and for the choices they make. This is the essence of principled parenting. It is a parent's *consistency* that produces an environment of *predictability*, and this contributes significantly to *stability* in the home.

Consistency + Predictability = Stability

When parents use this formula during the formative years, they help their kids come to own the age-appropriate choices they make, along with the consequences. The result is competent, confident kids. Note that competence comes first. When kids find an arena of competence (this includes gaming, skateboarding, jujitsu, or any other activity—including negative ones), this feeds their hearts and builds their confidence. Thus it is very important that we guide and direct kids toward healthy outlets that provide for competence ("I can do this"). These things will feed their confidence.

The Combination Effect

What's interesting about these parenting styles is that, to some degree, many parents take on all three throughout their child's life. For example, when kids are young (under age five), there isn't a great deal of verbal give-and-take. Sure, kids might be able to choose a particular outfit or shoes or play one game over another; but overall, parents are guiding the actions their kids take. As the children grow, most parents shift into a different parenting style that gives the child room to mature. This is an ebb-and-flow process. Those parents who don't allow for this give-and-take will encounter the most difficulties.

Fostering responsibility and independence in children's lives begins by recognizing you and your spouse's primary parenting style(s). Ultimately, how you parent your children will affect the way they handle rules and consequences. Parents, are you on the same parenting-style page as your spouse? Parenting inherently comes with conflicts along the way; however, these conflicts can be exacerbated when parents are at opposite ends of the parenting continuum, or when one parent takes on all or most of the parenting responsibilities.

The first step to fostering responsibility in kids is for parents to find common ground regarding how they parent. In fact, in my practice with parents, if a couple is unable to find common ground regarding rules, we end up spending most of our time working to resolve this. If they are unable to find common ground for addressing the primary issues, I've learned to back away from taking on those issues with their child. Why? Anytime parents implement or attempt to implement rules, there will be tension and sometimes conflict. If parents aren't on the same page, they can pretty much forget any effective changes taking place. The entire rules-and-consequences process begins with parents.

RULES ABOUT RULES: FOUR GUIDELINES

Major on the Majors, Not the Minors

Rules should be as few as possible. The objective of rules isn't to regulate every moment of your child's life, but to provide boundaries within which your child can make age-appropriate choices, demonstrate responsibility, and gain increasing independence. Your rules should point the way toward these objectives.

So what are the big-ticket items you need to address? When our daughter was in pre-K (four years old), her classroom teacher had three rules for the class of sixteen kids: be kind; be safe; do your job. That's it. What made these rules so effective was the teacher's daily reinforcement of these expectations, along with consistently applied consequences.

How about you? Do your kids know what the major rules are? Do they understand the consequences that will result should they choose to violate the rules?

When formulating the major rules, ask yourself what your child needs to move toward greater independence and responsibility? The whole purpose of your rules should be to help your kids gain additional freedoms as they demonstrate responsibility. If your rules don't bring this result, something is wrong, either with the consequence, your child's conscience, or both. If the issue is one of conscience, asking other caring adults (coaches, youth leaders, teachers, etc.) to speak into your child/teen's life can be beneficial. Working with your school's counselor is another good way to help them sort out the rationale for their behaviors.

The one caution I would offer is to be careful how you address the issue. The goal isn't conformity; it's to understand and develop the child's heart. Explain why the change is beneficial. This is about helping them see a better path for their own life. Neither is it about Mom and Dad wanting compliance; when kids believe this is the case, they often rebel even more. They must ultimately want to change for their own good, not for their parents. Finally, when the plan works, avoid any hint of making it seem like you won the battle. This is not about parental one-upmanship—it is about moving your kids toward greater independence and healthy life choices.

Make Rules as Clear as Possible

Confusing rules result in confusion for both parents and kids. When a rule is clearly delineated, your child is aware when they've broken it. They may try to cover it up, argue it didn't happen, or rationalize why it happened—but they know the rule was broken. When in doubt, clarify your expectations with examples: "Be at home by 8:00 p.m. *according to the clock in the living room*" is more clearly stated than "be home *at a reasonable hour.*"

When working with parents and kids in counseling settings, I often take on the role of a lawyer, arguing with a series of what-ifs. I encourage both parents and child to think of possible situations in which rules might be violated (curfew, owning your schoolwork, etc.). This exercise ensures that the child knows what will happen if they choose to violate a rule, even if the situation changes. I also ask the child to repeat the rules back to the parent. This means the parents know that the child knows what is expected, and the child knows that the parents know they know. If the rule is violated, the child won't be able to use the excuse: "I didn't know." To be sure, they may say "I forgot" or "I don't care," but they can't argue the point that they didn't know. Here's why this is important.

Parents must understand that kids have a strong tendency to want to create a plausible rationale that the choices they are making are somehow out of their control. They often do this so they can justify life happening to them, become passive, and take on the role of a victim of adolescence. While it's true that much of life is about learning and learning through error, parents must not allow kids to assume a passive/victim role when it comes to ownership of their choices. As long as kids are allowed to do this, then anything—and I mean *anything*—they do will be rationalized. Don't allow this to happen. Kids must step into ownership of the age-appropriate choices they are making. Then they will grow through the adversity and success, both of which come about as a result of the choices we allow them to own. Our job as parents is to provide the boundaries and then enable the kids to make decisions, all the while lovingly holding them accountable.

Write It Down and Sign It

When it comes to enforcing rules, emotions can run high. Kids may later forget or contend what they previously agreed to. For this reason, it's essential you write down the rules, including common excuses that might be used to negate the rules. Then, both parents and kids must sign the rule contract.

Remember, the purpose of rules is to increase the likelihood that your kids become more responsible, not less. If rules are merely about control and management, this process will break down.

I remember one dad discussing with his son what a clean room was supposed to look like. Point by point, he listed out on paper what it meant to have a clean room: pick up your laundry and put it in the dirty-clothes basket; hang up your towel; make your bed (showing him how); throw trash away; put all plates, cups, spoons, and forks in the kitchen; clean up the bathroom sink; straighten the shower curtain so it dries properly; clean desktops by putting books, papers, and pencils away. Once they'd put these rules in writing, there was no need for Dad to hover and micro-manage. He could just point to the agreement as needed.

In similar fashion, for each of the rules you implement, write out the specifics of what you are looking for. Once signed, this becomes the basis by which you enforce consequences. It is difficult to argue (but teens will) with something written down and signed by parents and kids.

The Buck Stops with You

Harry Truman, the thirty-third president of the United States, realized that the ultimate responsibility of "parenting" the executive branch of the government rested with him. He had to make difficult but necessary decisions to direct his large executive branch. On his presidential desk sat a placard in case anyone wondered who had the final say on matters. It read: *The buck stops here!* So too for parents—the buck stops with you.

When kids and parents can't come to a consensus on the rules, the parents' decision must be followed. Kids need parents who are assertive enough to make tough decisions and follow through with the consequences.

Parents sometimes tell me they feel like they are not their child's friend when they follow through with consequences or establish boundaries without compromising. Kids today grapple with complex issues such as character, schooling, premarital sex, and alcohol/drug use. Your kids don't need you to be their friend—they need you to be their parent. I would go so far as to say, if you want your kids to be your friend when they are older, make the tough calls today and stand united behind them. They will come to respect you and appreciate how you helped build their character.

It is in this difficult area where parents will be put to the test. Holding fast to the rules can be difficult when kids make parents feel bad for doing what they said they would do if the rule was violated. Kids will sulk, pout, become selectively mute, storm around the house, and display a full range of behaviors— all to make parents pay for holding fast to the rules.

I know of one eleven-year-old who refused to talk for three weeks when his parents took away his iPad because he'd violated the agreed-upon rule regarding its use. Sadly, some parents buckle, and his did. They came back to see me because parenting had become increasingly difficult. Before the incident, the three of us had talked about this rule, the rationale behind it, and what might result. We even role-played how their son might respond. They laughed at this, but when reality hit, it wasn't so funny. They had to redouble their efforts and forge ahead. They got through it and ended in a better place because of it, but it wasn't easy.

Much of the way parents learn is a result of trial and error— but we learn. When we stumble halfway through this process, it's okay to circle back and hit the redo button. This resolve is necessary for kids to understand their need for change. If our goal is to raise healthy, confident, independent kids, and the rules we formulate move the kids toward this goal, then no amount of cajoling should detract us from the process.

FOUR GUIDELINES FOR
FORMULATING AND ENFORCING CONSEQUENCES

Rules and consequences make up the two sides of a proverbial coin. Of the two, consequences are more difficult for parents to implement. As we've already said, however, rules without consequences are worthless. Simply put, if parents aren't prepared to follow through with consequences, they shouldn't merit out rules.

When parents don't stick with agreed-upon consequences, the entire process of fostering responsibility erodes. Kids know it's only a matter of manipulation for Mom and Dad to buckle. Moreover, kids perceive their parents as wimps. Kids are motivated to abide by the rules when they know there *will be* consistent consequences. Because kids employ a host of techniques to extract themselves from consequences (badgering, intimidation, threats, martyrdom, buttering up, physical tactics), parents must have an agreed-upon set of consequences they'll adhere to regardless of what measures kids employ to avoid them.

Establish Consequences at the Time Rules Are Formulated

Discuss with your child rules and consequences simultaneously. The value of agreeing upon predetermined consequences comes into play when rules are broken because both parents and kids already know what's going to happen. Parents don't have to be emotionally reactive, and kids won't be able to decry, "That's not fair!"

Be Consistent

Even though rules and consequences have been established, reality still happens. Parents, you are tired at the end of a long day of work. The last thing you want to do is contend with conflicts around rule violations, but an infraction has occurred. Because you've already established consequences, neither your emotional state nor your child's should dictate whether you carry out the consequences. You've made a commitment to see this process through. Of course, as with every facet of life, there should always be room for exceptions to consequences, but you, not your child, determine this.

Parents sometimes try, several times, to incorporate the steps noted above, yet experience limited success. In such times, it's easy to give up, saying, "We tried this, and it doesn't work." But before you give up on the plan, there are a few things you should consider.

Changing patterns of behavior is a difficult, time-consuming process. Expect conflict. Interestingly, even in areas of dysfunction, there's comfort in predictable routine. In fact, the older your child, the more difficult the process. Why? The family is accustomed to the patterns and routines Mom and Dad have allowed to develop. To change these patterns, parents must change the way they parent. Further, it can take twenty weeks (five months) of consistency to change behavior patterns in a teenager. The process is shorter with younger children, but it still takes consistent action. For example, for our eight-year-old and four-year-old, habit change took two to four weeks.

Carry Out Consequences Privately

Your children will need correction and reproof, but those moments shouldn't be considered lesson times for your other kids; neither should it be done in front of your child's peers. Think of it this way: how would you respond to a pugnacious boss who used shame-based tactics as a means of employee reproof? The unpleasant emotional responses you would probably undergo are similar to the ones your children will experience if this becomes your primary method for carrying out consequences. Remember, the purpose of carrying out consequences isn't to humiliate or shame, but to redirect, rebuild, and restore relationships.

Administer Consequences with Love

It's natural to become angry and frustrated when kids break rules, but this shouldn't be the primary emotion compelling your actions. The flip side is also true: Kids will resent parents who seem to take pleasure in administering consequences. If your child doesn't feel loved or if they view the rules and consequences as arbitrary and self-serving in your favor, they'll often rebel against the rule enforcers—their parents. Be kind but firm. We must love our kids enough to push, pull, tug, and hug them into adulthood. Sometimes love must be tough, but our kids should know we love them enough to parent them, even—and especially—in difficult circumstances.

Fostering responsibility and independence in kids' lives is an evolving activity. As your children mature and grow, your rules and consequences for them should as well.

FAQs

What's the best way to introduce young children to responsibility in the home? Parents sometimes think that younger children (ages four to eight) can't do much with respect to taking on household responsibilities. I also hear that having hired help in the home (not uncommon for families overseas) makes it difficult for kids to learn responsibility. In either case, with proper guidance and accountability, even young children can participate in chores around the home.

Both of our children have household responsibilities. They make their beds each morning and get themselves ready for school. In addition to these responsibilities, our twelve-year-old sets the dinner table, and our eight-year-old clears it. Our eight-year-old began this task when she was four. Before this, our twelve-year-old cleared the table, starting at age six. He's now ready to take on additional responsibilities. He also feeds the cat daily and provides water for her. They both must clean up their rooms before meals.

We don't run a militant home, but we do have expectations that we've consistently reinforced, and this has made all the difference. Our younger child has had opportunities to observe what's happening with her older brother. She is learning vicariously as she sees how we lovingly hold him accountable for his age-appropriate choices. These kid-level responsibilities aren't optional. They are requirements that our kids fulfill as members of the family. Interestingly, we've had little in the way of objections, primarily because the kids make predictions as to what will happen if they choose to neglect these responsibilities. The predictions are based on our years of consistency. In order for our kids to learn these tasks, we had to first model, then teach, coach, and guide them. After a few weeks of feedback, they understood what the expectations were and followed through.

Putting toys away after playing can begin as early as two years of age. Make it a game; when moving on to a new activity, we make sure to clean up, but it doesn't have to be a tedious chore. We even found a song that made it more fun, and the kids responded accordingly. Along the way, we have learned many parenting techniques from parents who have gone before us.

My wife and I continue to learn and grow as parents. We have and still do spend a considerable amount of time talking with parents of older children who've raised great kids to help us understand what lies ahead. In my work with parents, I'm privileged to hear hundreds of stories about what works and why. We incorporate the principles these parents share that correspond to our values into how we parent. I encourage you to do the same. Surround yourself with parents who have raised well-adjusted kids—kids who are grown or at least ahead of yours in terms of age or stages. Ask them how did they did it. Ask for suggestions and recommendations. Ask, seek, learn.

Parents with children ages three to ten can consider the following chores: room tidiness, hygiene, getting dressed, clearing and setting the table, helping wash/dry dishes, taking out the garbage, and helping carry in the groceries. The key in this entire process is for parents to be consistent. To aid in this, find out what motivates your kids. Then, when necessary, leverage this to aid in the process. For our kids, leverage includes desserts, TV time, iPad use, and play dates. Rarely have we had to restrict or remove these, but we have and will when necessary.

Mealtime has become a battleground. Our kids complain about what we've made, argue about what they should eat, and mope when we force them to finish eating. What advice would you offer? My wife remembers conflict between her brother and parents over mealtimes, particularly about him eating whatever was put on his plate. We didn't want this conflict to be part of our parenting, but we did want our kids to eat what was placed before them.

We decided to stick to a simple, consistent plan: If our children didn't want to eat what we placed before them, they would not be offered anything else to eat for the rest of the evening, nor would they be allowed to have dessert. If the conflict occurred at breakfast or lunch, they would not be allowed to have between-meal snacks. That's it. If they whine, complain, or cause a fuss, we don't get angry, yell, or bribe. We simply excuse them from the table to go to their rooms, so the rest of us can enjoy our meal and the company of one another.

To sweeten the deal, we usually have great desserts. Our eight-year-old has gotten to the point where she asks what's for dessert before she decides if she is going to eat all her dinner. She understands the rule and consciously makes the choice. She knows she will not get any additional food for the rest of the night or between meals, but we allow her to make this choice.

I should point out, we do make allowances. There are food items I'm more drawn to than others. I dislike olives, but my wife and daughter like them. You can give leeway when it comes to the amounts and types of food kids eat, but don't base those decisions on a child's emotional state.

Any advice on how I can I help my younger child with their schooling? I'm concerned they aren't working up to their potential. At the start of the school year, counselors and administrators occasionally find moms wandering the halls of the primary division (kindergarten through second grade), peering into classroom windows, peeking behind cement pillars, and attempting to follow their child from class to class. Many parents experience anxiety when it comes to little ones, primarily because they believe if their child is trailing other students socially, emotionally, or academically, they are to blame. To compensate, some parents enroll their three- and four-year-olds in enrichment courses, arrange for tutors, and conduct parental study sessions. By the time these parents meet with me, they've usually reached a stage of exhaustion, frustration, or extreme apprehension. Despite all their efforts, they believe their child is not reaching their full potential.

Once I'm reasonably confident there aren't significant academic, social, or emotional issues, I try to help parents understand what their role could be. I suggest ways they can create an environment for learning and allow their child ownership of it. This is difficult work. Parents must resist the tendency to tie the quality of their child's performance to the quality of their parenting. This is a primary contributor to parental anxiety.

Primary parental roles during the formative years include directing and providing assistance with study habits as well as coaching and modeling social and emotional skills. Kids need parental guidance. What this means academically, for example, is that parents help to establish study routines and patterns. Once established, it will be important to partner with the teacher to reinforce academic expectations. Teachers can play a significant role in this regard, yet far too few parents consult with them. Instead, they seek out tutors or meet with psychologists or school counselors. Yikes! The starting point for understanding your child's learning *begins* with the teacher(s).

When working with parents who are worried about their child's learning (regardless of age or grade), I begin my investigation with the teacher. In 80 percent of the cases, this is where my investigation ends. I gain far more insight into a child's learning from their teacher reporting day-to-day functioning than I do from any diagnostic tool. Functional (day-to-day) progress is the single most important source of information for understanding a child's learning. Breakdowns (academic, social, or emotional) are generally the result of too little guidance, structure, or support or, conversely, too much ownership of these by the parent. The process continually ebbs and flows as children mature. When not addressed consistently, any ongoing conflict will increase in intensity.

By the time a child reaches middle school, I strongly encourage parents to back away from being the primary persons for making sure the child is performing the necessary academic responsibilities. If the work of parents has been carried out consistently up to this point, in most cases, kids will be able to handle the academic, age-appropriate expectations. This does not mean parents are on easy street. Much is still required by way of expectation and accountability. Young teens will need ongoing support and structure, but it should be implemented with the goal of increasing the child's independence. In formulating support, ask yourself if what you are presently doing will lead your child to be more independent and responsible. If you're unsure, consult your child's teacher or counselor.

What are some primary issues I should be aware of when it comes to raising teens? The primary areas where parents will need to help their teenagers include:

- Schooling (homework/grades)
- Electronic devices: computers, cell phones, tablets, gaming systems
- Drugs and Alcohol
- Dating/sex
- Character issues
- Respecting others, both at home and school
- Regulating emotions

To illustrate an approach parents might take, consider the first issue: schooling (homework/grades). The most frequent type of meeting I have with parents involves their child's academic progress. The area of academic performance can turn a home into a tinderbox. When parents demand academic excellence and kids proclaim, "I'm working as hard as I can," conflict is bound to occur. I recommend parents focus on the process and leave the grade talk alone. If parents and kids reach an impasse, I concentrate on three areas by asking the following questions of their teachers. Note: The questions are not for parents or students; they seek the objective, third-party input of the teacher.

- Is the student working to the best of his/her ability as defined by their teacher? What is the quality of the student's work, relative to what it was when they began in the class? Does the teacher see improvement? Are they making an effort to participate? If not, why? What does the teacher see happening? In short, is the trajectory of their learning moving in a positive direction?
- Is the student turning in their work on time? This question is not about the quality of the work; that's part of the first question. My only concern with this question is whether they are turning in their work on time. This has to do with organization, ownership, and time management.
- Does the student have a positive attitude toward learning? Is their attitude positive while attending class? Do they work

well with other kids? If not, why? What is the teacher seeing concerning their attitude toward learning?

If one or more of the above areas are out of sync, then parents should hold their child accountable and expect more from them. If, however, the child is working to the best of their ability, is getting their work turned in on time, and has a positive attitude, my advice to parents is to back off from the you-can-do-better conversation. Continuing to make academic demands (usually with threats thrown in) will ultimately lead to futility, frustration, and conflict.

When parents continue to press me to help their child after I've gone through these initial steps and noted no major concerns from teachers, I inform them that I won't be party to pressuring their child to improve academically. If, however, one of these areas is out of sync, you can bet I'll help address concerns. Some kids will only earn B and C grades (i.e., approaching or meeting expectations). Not every kid will receive high marks in every academic area. Acceptance of this doesn't mean the parent is admitting defeat or letting things go. It's about choosing where to devote one's parental energies. Keep in mind that, for some kids, learning is really hard work! Finding a balance by using the above questions as a guide will help parents when addressing issues of learning, all the while supporting and nurturing a growing young heart.

What are your thoughts about limiting computer and phone time? When my son was in second grade (eight years old) he began asking me to view his blog. His teacher told us a blog would be a good way to keep track of his writings and topics of interest. She went on to say, "This will become his digital portfolio, showcasing his growth and development as a writer throughout his schooling." Did you get that? An eight-year-old-kid—my kid—was leaving a digital footprint of his thoughts, ideas, and writings—one that will follow him throughout his schooling and life! Maybe I'm "old school" (a person over forty, as defined by my students), but this strikes me as Orwellian. My second grader, however, loved it.

Computers and cell phones are as pervasive in educational

settings as they are in the workplace. Schools are assigning laptops to kids as early as sixth grade (age eleven), with the expectation they will act responsibly—typically with little on-going guidance. Unless parents enforce, monitor, and model appropriate use of technology, this won't happen.

Technology is a tool and, like any tool, without proper training, it can quickly lead to unintended consequences. I define technology here as anything that plugs in or runs on batteries and entices kids. If you allow your children access to technology without boundaries and guidance, you can and should expect trouble.

For kids in middle school and below (grade eight, age thirteen or younger), I would not advocate access to a dedicated computer without monitoring software and parental controls. There are too many places online for kids to be enticed. Issues with online and offline character, bullying, balance in all areas of time management including screen time, as well as posting and/or viewing inappropriate content are but a few of the countless topics that should be addressed throughout these formative years. As kids/teens demonstrate responsibility, additional technological freedoms should be granted.

For kids age fourteen and older, I recommend parents set a designated, age-appropriate time by which the teen's computer, phone, and other electronic devices are removed from their room and placed in a central location where they charge for the night. While parents can't force teens to sleep, they can set up an environment more conducive to that goal. Working back from "lights out," have your child set up a schedule for what they need to accomplish, knowing "lights out" is approaching. Most kids will have three to four hours at home after dinner to finish their schoolwork.

If your teen habitually contests the curfew, investigate how they are spending their time online. Most likely you will find they are on social networks, texting, gaming, watching movies, and/or listening to music, all at the same time. Add to this the English paper due tomorrow, and you can pretty much forget about any schoolwork being completed on time or in good order.

Begin dealing with this issue by using available parental controls or installing monitoring software on their computers that keep a log of what they are doing online. These tools help parents communicate with their teen(s) in many ways. Imagine how your conversation would change if you could show your teen that last week they spent ten hours on YouTube, watching video clips of people flipping a half-filled bottle of water? They might protest that they were only watching it in the background and not on it all the time, but they couldn't deny the reality that it was open for ten hours.

Add to this any additional time spent elsewhere on Snapchat, Instagram, Skype, or other media running in the background, and very quickly one could build a case that time management and self-control are major issues that must be addressed before any additional online time will be allotted. If they can't sort this out, then you will need to step in and restrict access to these sites until they begin to make better choices around self-regulation.

For many teens, the use of technology isn't an issue. These kids have learned (operative word) to use their time online appropriately and responsibly. I would not advise parents to implement restrictions where they are not needed. I would, however, have frequent conversations around what others are doing that's not so great. I would also continue to require a mandatory "no technology in rooms past a certain hour."

What are your thoughts on kids and alcohol use? Teens drink primarily to cope. Parents, don't forget this! Teens use alcohol and/or drugs to cope with their experiences. They may be trying to fit in, de-stress, forget, or deal with hurt, frustration, or anger. I've dedicated Chapter 19 to addressing this topic. For now, let me say, the longer parents can keep their kids from drinking, the less likely they are to have alcohol abuse issues as adults.

What do you think is an appropriate age for teens to begin dating? According to a 2015 Centers for Disease Control and Prevention survey, approximately 59 percent of high school students surveyed indicated they have not had sexual intercourse.[1] That means approximately 41 percent have had sex. If you were to ask me when it's appropriate for my son or daughter to date, my reply would be, "sometime around thirty!" Seriously speaking, I don't see much good happening when kids begin dating before sixteen. I am in favor of providing healthy opportunities for kids to mix in groups and socialize, but dating prior to the age of sixteen, I am not.

I remember sitting in my office when a sixteen-year-old boy loped in and slumped down on my couch without speaking. (Every school psychologist should have a good couch.) He looked like he had just seen a ghost. I'd seen this look before; it's common among teenagers. After sitting for a few moments and collecting his thoughts, he said, "Girls. I mean, you know, girls! How do you know when you have met *the one*?" For the next hour, we discussed love, rejection, anxiety, and a host of other emotions commonly associated with feeling "in love" (or infatuation). Parents, do you remember feeling this way for the first time? Do you remember the intensity of emotions, the mountaintop experiences, and the all-too-common, crash-and-burn feelings associated with falling in love for the first time? Your kids will experience these emotions as well.

Sadly, we live in a sexualized culture, one in which increasingly younger kids are bombarded by a media that portrays sex as commonplace or a rite of passage. Into these areas parents must wage cultural war. Have conversations early and often, beginning around age nine. You needn't discuss all the issues at once, but you must broach the topic. As kids get older, help them understand sex isn't merely a biological process, a feeling, or a drive; teach them the moral implications as well.

"Don't have sex until you're married" may be an antiquated stance, but there is wisdom behind this adage. Others will be critical of this view, even parents of young teens, noting that if two people love each other, then sexual activity shouldn't be thought of as wrong. I respectfully and ardently disagree. I've seen the outworking of this thinking far too often. The pregnant teen faced with the dilemma of having a child or an abortion. A teen who was promised love forever, but the lover is no longer present. Talk about setting up a kid for a world of heartache. No thanks. I'll continue to pitch my tent in the abstinence camp.

I'm not so naïve to think the temptation of sexual activity isn't present in kids' lives. My wife and I will be intentional and proactive in conversing with our children regarding why we're opposed to sex *outside of marriage*. The issue isn't sex itself; rather, it's the implications, the deeper meaning of what sex conveys, and the consequences of engaging in sexual activity outside the bounds of a committed, marital relationship.

How about you? Have you had conversations with your kids about sex? Please don't leave this to the schools, older siblings, or the media. This is a crucial time for parental guidance; make your voice heard. I recently signed a permission slip for my eleven-year-old to attend a series of school-sponsored talks regarding sex. You can bet I'll be following up on these conversations! These talks are happening earlier and earlier. Parents need to be in front of these conversations if they are to expect a measure of credibility with their kids. Again, don't leave this to the school, the media, their peers, or even another relative. Mom and Dad, you must actively engage here.

15

From Teenagers to Screenagers[1]

There are three kinds of death in this world.
There's heart death, there's brain death,
and there's being off the network.

GUY ALMES

When I was in seventh grade, a friend of mine received a Mattel electronic football game from his parents. The year was 1983, and the electronic gaming revolution was taking hold. Soon after, other games followed: Space Invaders, Asteroids, Cold War Missile Command, Tempest, and Pac-Man, to name a few. By today's standards, we would be considered "gamers." These games didn't occupy our time; they cannibalized it, and we wouldn't have had it any other way. By the time I was in the latter part of high school, however, the games had lost much of their appeal. Still, there were a few kids who continued to game all throughout high school—and beyond.

ﾞﾐ

Today's teens have grown up with the internet. Much of their social life seems dependent on devices that enable them to stay connected to people and media. In fact, their lives are so bound up in their electronic devices that some have coined the term *screenagers* to describe them. Screenagers primarily keep in touch with friends and family through texting, social networking, email, blogs, and websites. They spend much of their time in front of screens of various sizes—from cell phones and video game consoles to laptop computers and high-definition televisions. A report by the Kaiser Family Foundation noted that the total amount of leisure time American kids devote to media/technology is on par with a full-time job.[2]

125

An interesting characteristic of screenagers is their purported efficiency at multitasking. There has been much hype regarding this perceived advantage; however, looking more closely at this phenomenon gives rise to many concerns. Dr. David Meyer, University of Maryland, notes, "Switching back and forth from one task to another takes its toll. As you're switching, you are not concentrating on either task."[3]

While teens can access more information than previous generations, the quality of thinking that goes into determining the validity of the content is often shallow. Kids wander around the internet in search of *facts* without a foundation for determining what's *factual*. An essential skill, therefore, is knowing where to look online and analyzing what's found. Sadly, the phrase "click, copy, paste" depicts a portion of the academic work screenagers produce. This may explain why sites such as TurnItIn.com have seen a marked rise in popularity among those in academia.[4] Using a student's submitted paper, TurnItIn scours the internet, locating sentences, quotes, paragraphs, and full papers students have stolen and credited to themselves. The site compiles this information and generates a report for the teacher that shows all suspected areas of the student's work. The use of such tools among educators isn't so much to catch kids cheating. Rather, it's to help educate students on the importance of producing their own work in the process of evaluating others.

Another interesting developmental aspect of screenagers is their lack of patience. As if it's a form of digital etiquette, they expect replies to texts or email messages immediately. Waiting is perceived as a form of disrespect, disinterest, or outright rejection. Never mind the reality that the recipient of said text or email might be engaged in some other pressing matter. When the phone vibrates or the email bell chimes, all other activities must cease (so much for dinner). It should come as little surprise that a Nielsen study of 65,000 teens, ages thirteen through seventeen, discovered that on average, each teen sends 3,417 texts per month (approximately 2,815 texts for boys and 3,952 for girls).[5] For many parents, texting has become a primary tool of communication between them and their child, and this is just fine with teens. Richard Watson, the author of *Future Minds*, humorously describes cell phones as "proximity devices allowing teens to reshape time and space."[6] And indeed they are.

DIGITALLY DISCIPLINED

When it comes to raising kids in a wired world, the challenge parents and educators face is helping them become digitally disciplined. Discipline in this sense not only involves training, correcting, and molding mental faculties, but also moral character. Parents spend incalculable hours instructing children on moral and ethical responsibilities and duties, yet are they doing the same when it comes to digital discipline? With these thoughts in mind, I have two suggestions for parents.

Know What Your Kids Are Doing Online

By the time you turn the knob on your screenager's bedroom door, their fingers have already moved into overdrive, minimizing windows and closing objectionable sites. The reality is, many parents have no idea what kids are doing online. If you're finding the computer is consuming the majority of your screenager's free time and this is contributing to conflict in the home, then you owe it to yourselves to see what they are doing. I can assure you: it's not all homework. For some families, monitoring software may be a necessary option. Check out Top Ten Reviews (http://monitoring-software-review.toptenreviews.com/) for a listing of software and reviews. Monitoring software is easy to download and can greatly aid in understanding your child's online activities. If you're not monitoring what your kids are doing with social media and technology, then you're partly responsible for the conflict.

Institute Digital Downtime

When was the last time you sat down as a family for dinner and didn't have text messages or various chimes interrupting your meal? Traditionally, the dinner table has served as a great place for reconnecting family members, a place where families gather to discuss events of the day. However, with a bajillion electronic devices competing for our attention, parents may consider instituting a no-tech table policy such as: "If it plugs in or runs on batteries, don't bring it to the dinner table." This is a rule for everyone, including parents.

A colleague and friend shared this next idea with me, and I

think it's a great one. Make it a rule that all family members keep their cell phones and laptop computers in one central location before going to bed. Many screenagers sleep with their phones in hand, not wanting to miss the most recent status update, tweet, or text. If you're attempting to promote disconnect time and balance, I recommend a traditional alarm clock. It is common practice for teens and adults to use the alarm feature on their phones, but for the teen struggling with online balance this may not be the best option.

If having trouble unplugging from devices describes your teen, they already have issues with balancing their priorities. Back up, make new plans, and reboot the system. If they resist, stop paying their cell phone bill. Yes, they will experience the painful effects of withdrawal, but there's a bigger principle you are trying to impart, namely a balanced life.

KEEPING THE BALANCE

As new technologies are brought forth, parents must stay connected as well, and must do so in such a way that kids recognize that responsibility extends into the reaches of cyberspace. We are in the midst of an educational/technological revolution. Now is not the time for parental retreat. Instead, parents must become increasingly engaged. Seek for yourselves understanding and clarification of why and how digital tools can aid or potentially harm the development of young minds.

In many respects, we're living faster than we are thinking. While we relish the speed of communication, it sometimes forces us to respond without thinking. Keeping a balance is about dialogue, discussion, reflection, and yes, discipline; however, without your involvement, this won't happen. According to Richard Watson, schools and homes should embrace digital learning "but they should primarily celebrate their physical spaces and the people, objects, and artifacts contained within them."[7]

FAQs

Do you really think today's social media tools are addictive?
It's not uncommon to hear terms such as *addiction* and *dependency* referenced when describing those who play online

games or other electronic media. When it comes to the concerns parents raise regarding their child's gaming, psychologists frame questions around the follow terms: *salience, mood alteration, tolerance, withdrawal, conflict,* and *relapse.*[8] To a greater or lesser degree, these terms help define the level of the problem.

- *Salience.* As an activity, how important is gaming in a person's life? Does gaming dominate their thinking and behaviors? For example, even when a person is not online, are most of their conversations, thoughts, and actions geared toward their next gaming experience?
- *Mood alteration.* How does a person feel as a result of gaming? Some people experience a high or feelings of euphoria because of gaming, while others feel despondent between gaming sessions.
- *Tolerance.* Are increasing amounts of gaming required to achieve the desired mood-altering effects? For some, this is a gradual build up. For others, it morphs from one platform (game style) to another.
- *Withdrawal symptoms.* When required or requested to cease their gaming, does the person experience protracted moodiness and irritability?
- *Conflict.* Are there significant and pervasive difficulties in other areas of their lives (i.e., schoolwork, household responsibilities, job, other interests) as a result of gaming?
- *Relapse.* Have there been reversions to earlier patterns of behavior despite attempts to stop?

If you have concerns with your child's gaming, take proactive steps. This may include speaking with your child's counselor, seeking outside counseling or school assistance, and instituting parental controls on your child's computer.

What are your thoughts on monitoring software? Monitoring software affords parents the opportunity to track or monitor their child's online activity. Parents often ask this question on the heels of being frustrated with their child's use of social media. Their desire isn't so much to restrict use as it is to regulate it. Finding the sweet spot for balance is a difficult task. Ideally, this process should begin at an early age (as soon as they have access), but much of the time it doesn't. In my clinical work, I've noticed that parents often assume their kids can handle the responsibility of online management on their own. Many can't, and this is what gets them into trouble.

Also, please know this isn't a question of good kid/bad kid. Some temptations are simply bigger than kids can manage. When their competition for completing schoolwork is Facebook, Snapchat, Netflix, YouTube, gaming, and so on, it's no wonder that kids don't always get their work completed.

Begin by placing boundaries around a child's use of technology. For example, in our home, the kids (now ages eight and twelve) understand they can only be online for recreational purposes during the weekends. During school nights, they may have computer-related homework, but this is monitored. They are only allowed to access apps related to their schoolwork.

When working with families who have children struggling with online management, our first suggestion, most often, is to set up parental controls on the kid's computer or smartphone.

If your child has a Mac/Apple laptop, you can quickly set up parental controls to regulate the amount of time their computer will be on during the day/evening. If you go to YouTube and type "parental controls for Apple" (or whatever your device is), you will find scores of online videos providing step-by-step instructions on how to set these up. You can also use parental controls for smartphones.

In phase one of the process, we may choose only to monitor where the student is going online without regulating time and use. Why? Often teens note they are spending hours doing homework. Translation: They don't have time to come out of their room for supper, must stay up late to study, can't go with the family for dinner, and so on. When you review where they have been online, however, a different story unfolds. The software helps you recover their history (where they've been online), and you can quickly determine the truth of what they are asserting. In most cases, they are indeed doing *some* schoolwork, but not nearly the amount they claim. Should they choose not to regulate their time on their own, parents can then step in and restrict it.

Phase two of this process includes setting a definitive cut-off time when the computer turns off each night. Kids must self-regulate to complete their school tasks and manage their social media usage. If they are unable to do this, then parents may take the next step and eliminate the use of certain heavily trafficked social media sites. This can be done with parental controls as well. Simply type in the websites that will be restricted, and it's done.

It's important to remember that a smartphone can perform all the functions of a laptop. In fact, most kids use their phone as their primary means of accessing the internet. Be sure to set up and monitor controls on this piece of technology as well.

Again, the goal isn't to be punitive but to help your child take ownership of their learning, emotions, and schedules. Many parents also struggle with this and should be able to empathize. What's more, the process will feel like we're trying to hit a moving target. As soon as we sort out an issue, the kids grow and we must move the boundary. Not doing so leads to additional conflict. We grow, we learn, we move forward.

Do you think it's okay for my teen to have a computer in their room? Deciding to allow a computer in a teen's room depends on whether they have demonstrated age-appropriate responsibility. Through the years, have you been able to trust and verify they are doing what's expected with technology? Do they become increasingly agitated when you ask them to be involved in family activities? Is your parental instinct kicking in, telling you something isn't right?

How you answer these questions will determine which steps to take. If your kid is responsible with technology, then there is no need to micromanage. If they aren't, you need to intervene. Regardless of age and demonstrated responsibility, I strongly recommend computers and phones come out of kids' rooms at a certain time each night. If you want to improve your child's sleeping habits, this is a must. Have a central docking station where all technology charges each night.

What if my teen is sneaky with his phone and I catch him with it in his room on several occasions? If you've communicated your concerns regarding technology in their room (balance, sleep, scheduling, family time, etc.), and they persist in being untrustworthy, take the phone away for a week.

What if my child can't be trusted with a computer, but the school says they need one? Many schools do require kids to have access to computers as a part of their learning. On the surface, this may present itself as a severe obstacle, but it can be worked out. Contact your child's counselor and teachers; inform them of the conflicts taking place, and they will assist. A few weeks with a notebook and pen will teach your child to make different choices.

What if my child refuses to turn over their smartphone? Most kids would prefer you take their right foot rather than disconnect them from social media. If you've reached this point and need to take further action, you can always have their phone disconnected. Being disconnected from friends is akin to being dead these days. I do recommend this step as a last resort. At my present school, for example, we have required certain students to turn in their phones at the start of the school day. They can pick them up at the end of the day. In the interim, they need to figure out how to navigate relationships without the use of technology.

What additional thoughts do you have about technology? Helping kids understand the decisions we make with technology is part of the work of parenting. Like kids, adults also struggle with time management. Technology is only one of many choices grownups manage daily. What example are we setting for them? Showing our kids that we understand the draw to these devices can help them understand our interest in teaching them these management skills.

Technology is increasingly interconnected to learning. For this reason, I encourage parents to get involved, stay active, and not resign themselves to apathy.

Lastly, technology is a tool. It's not good or bad; it's neutral. How we use it—both parents and kids—determines if it's helpful or hurtful. Some parents have pulled all technology away, believing it's harmful to kids. So too is candy, soda, and chips—in excess. The reality is, our kids are going to own these platforms going forward; much of what they will do as adults will involve technology. They are looking to their parents for guidance. Just as you will need to teach them to drive a car, you will need to teach them to navigate social media. Stay active, get involved, and seek to understand.

16

Game On

*The good news about computers is that they do
what you tell them to do. The bad news is that
they do what you tell them to do.*

TED NELSON

Dimly lit lights, half empty pizza boxes, and the thunderous sounds of cheers and groans filter their way from the television room throughout the house. Entering the room, you notice Stephen and his friends engaged in what appears to be a series of technologically orchestrated electronic sequences involving an ergonomically designed handheld device and the television.

What is going on here?

૨&

Whether you're speaking of today's sophisticated and highly interactive gaming systems or the arcade machines historically found in malls and pubs, electronic games have become a mainstay of our culture. The *New York Times* reports Americans spend more money on video games than they do on movies.[1] Worldwide sales of video game consoles and software are expected to reach \$98 billion by 2020.[2] That's more than twice the revenue of the National Football League, National Basketball Association, and Major League Baseball combined![3] Gaming is no longer child's play but a lucrative economic enterprise.

With such economic numbers driving the market, gaming no longer comprises a subset of the culture; it has become embedded in and is a large part of the mainstream. Researchers Beck and Wade note, "Games are a technology universally adopted by a large, young cohort and ignored by their elders."[4]

For kids today, gaming is everywhere, established, emotionally enticing, and part of the fabric of their lives. Kids don't know of a time when gaming didn't exist. As far as they are concerned, people who didn't grow up with such *necessities* might as well have been born hundreds of years ago—and sometimes this is how parents feel. Part of the difficulty is that parents who were born before 1985 have had comparatively limited experience gaming as children. Without this reference point, these parents may be at a loss to appreciate their allurement. Alternatively, many of the parents born after this period were the original players from whom today's gaming community evolved. They most likely have gaming experience, but they may not understand the pervasiveness of the issue. With today's online communities, gaming has left the four walls of the home and is virtually unlimited.

Bring It On

While it is true that games are a consumer product, they are also a consumer experience. A central feature of games is that they draw on parts of reality, while simultaneously drawing on powerful emotions. Games put the players in direct control of various scenarios. Whether the character is a soldier fighting in WWII or a wizard casting spells, the outcome is ultimately in the hands of the person with the controls. Video games provide a platform where kids can fulfill the urge to challenge, compete, and win, without leaving a permanent record of failures.

The physical skills for gaming on the surface appear quite simple—hitting the right sequence of buttons at the right moment. But these skills can be taken to extremely high levels. Wins and losses aren't evaluated solely based on a score but an acquisition of a new skill or level of understanding. Gaming is progressive in nature. With each additional game played, a new level of understanding and confidence is gained. Gratification and tangible improvement can be charted moment by moment, game by game. One would be hard pressed to replicate this type of continuous reinforcement in other areas of life, including the classroom.

In her book, *The Psychology of the Internet*, Patricia Wallace notes, "We are in an age when attention is a commodity in short supply but very great [in] demand."[5] This is one factor that makes gaming so appealing and possibly compulsive.

I'm the Hero

The world of reality takes a backseat when it comes to gaming. Games are all about role-playing. Players assume the role of a soldier, pilot, sorcerer, athlete, or one of a host of other characters. The characteristics of gaming also trigger a wide assortment of half-truths and exaggerations. Gaming allows kids to try on different roles and interact with others who have similar interests and abilities, even while it insulates them from the consequences of their actions. This form of social interaction and development is markedly different from experiences commonly noted by parents when they were kids.

Children of past generations typically formed bonds with others based on schools they attended and club, sport, or religious affiliations. While this is still true of kids today, the phenomenon of online gaming affords the opportunity to connect with others and develop a sense of belonging and community, even if this community is electronically based.

Gaming also makes it possible for kids, regardless of physical and social limitations, to become the central hero of their virtual world. It puts them at the center of a universe where the world—albeit a virtual one—does indeed revolve around them.

Social Enticements

In computer gaming, a Multi-User Domain (MUD) is a multi-player computer game combining elements of role-playing and instant messaging. People connected to the internet from anywhere in the world become part of a team working toward an established goal, all along the way communicating with one another via a dialogue box that is part of the game itself. For example, in EverQuest (a popular MUD), players explore a Tolkienesque fantasy world of swords and sorcery, fighting monsters and enemies for treasure and experience points, all the while interacting with other players. As they progress, players advance in levels gaining power, prestige, and increased abilities. Also, players may opt to take part in battles against other players, including both duels and fights against player characters allied with an enemy faction.

Entering this gaming area can be likened to meeting up with friends for a night on the town. When gaming, kids form friendships with others with whom they may share no other interest (or physical proximity); however, the bonds formed through these interactions can be just as intense and significant as any other relationship.

Teens are in the process of asking the fundamental question "Who am I?" Along the way, games help them to express and explore several aspects of this question. Over the course of adolescence, teens address substantial developmental tasks including healthy, positive relationships with peers and developing an understanding of social forms and norms. Online gaming draws teens toward others—even on an international platform—where they can communicate, interact, and share similar experiences. These experiences influence who the teen will become.

Worst-Case Scenarios

At what point, if at all, should gaming become a concern? I frequently meet with parents who are concerned about the amount of time their children spend gaming. They wonder at what point they should intervene, but therein lies a significant difficulty. Controversy still surrounds the extent to which gaming behavior is considered addictive or compulsive, both for laypeople and psychologists. We have little to go on at this juncture other than anecdotes, a few surveys, and societal concerns over the impact excessive gaming is having on some kids' lives; however, the body of evidence is growing.

Director of Computer Addiction Services at Harvard University-affiliated McLean Hospital, Dr. Orzak, believes social aspects are a primary factor in compulsive gaming. He notes, "Many people are lonely, have never felt like they belonged.... People get a sense of belonging in the game. In some cases, it provides the only friends they interact with."[6]

As a starting point, some general areas for parents to consider regarding possible excessive use of gaming include:

- Lifestyle changes that allow more time for gaming.
- General decreases in physical activity, instead devoting

additional time to gaming.

- A disregard for one's health (missing meals) and hygiene in order to game.
- Avoiding homework or social obligations in order to game.
- A decrease in socializing, resulting in loss of friends due to gaming behaviors.
- Craving for more time at the computer and becoming agitated if prohibited from gaming.
- Changes in sleep patterns, including sleep deprivation, to spend additional time gaming.

The symptoms noted above are by no means exhaustive, nor are they official criteria for gaming addiction or compulsive gaming. In fact, no official psychological or psychiatric diagnosis for gaming or internet addiction has gained consensus among mental health providers; however, countries like South Korea and China have established criteria.

Gamers and the games they play are rapidly evolving. As the ink dries on this chapter, new gaming platforms are being launched and new games are hitting the market. The challenge before parents is to keep up with these changes and to be aware of the factors shaping and influencing the way children think. In other words, it's time to get in the game.

FAQs

I'm pretty sure my son has a problem with gaming. The amount of time he's spending online, the conflicts, the apathy when we speak with him about regulating his time—all are for naught. What should we do? Accounts like this raise the hairs on my neck. Many conflicts will be faced in the process of dialing back this child's amount of gaming. As a starting point, I would determine what reinforcement he/she (most likely he) is getting through gaming. Is it affiliation, a sense of accomplishment, dominance, control, or some combination of all these? Ideally, I would help them find socially acceptable ways to supplement gaming.

Some readers may contend that the best approach would be to pull the plug altogether and just let the child deal with it. This action could be taken, but it's not one I would initially endorse.

To some degree, parents have created this problem by not establishing boundaries and guidelines. Removing the technology without understanding the attraction and then trying to dial things back is command-control parenting. This approach isn't about what's best for the child; it's an attempt at a quick fix for a problem parents have helped create by not setting appropriate boundaries.

I would begin by placing limits on what the child is doing online. I would also try to gain an understanding of their draw to be online. What are they lacking that gaming provides? For example, if they are known in the digital arena as powerful, confident, and in control, what could the parent do to help foster these attributes in the real world? In what ways can the parent point out, in civil conversations, their concerns and help them to establish new norms? Be specific, provide guidance, and move forward. Speaking with other parents or the child's school counselor may also be a good way to gain understanding as to the "why" behind their gaming.

My eleven-year-old is becoming increasingly interested in technology. I feel like he is being coaxed into a world I know little about. To be candid, I feel like I'm trying to hold back something I have little control over. What should I do? In some ways, I share your sentiments. It seems like technology is all encompassing, dehumanizing our kids—but this isn't the case. If parents take the time to understand what is happening with technology, how kids are utilizing it, and what they are gaining from it, they will be less worried and more empowered to step into their role as parents to guide their children. Fear of the unknown contributes to the anxiety. I encourage parents to begin asking themselves questions around balance and boundaries.

Don't fall for the misconception that, because your child needs a computer for school, you really can't do anything about it. You can do something. You can help them regulate and manage what they do and where they go online. As we've discussed, you can set boundaries around technology use in the home, where they study online, when the cut-off time is, and more.

I find it somewhat strange that my kids enjoy watching videos of people playing video games. They could spend hours doing this. What's going on here? I recently shared this observation with a group of parents asking, "How many of you can relate to this parent's comments?" Most of the parents in the room raised their hands and laughed. They found it humorous. One astute parent in the audience spoke into the humor to remind folks they do this as well. He went on to ask, "How many of you have played tennis, football, basketball, or other sports, and then watched others on TV play the same games?" For the first time, many understood the connection. Kids watch and imitate (play) that which they are interested in. As adults, we take little pleasure in watching countless videos of others playing games because we lack a context or reference point for understanding. If we played some of these games, my guess is we would watch some of those videos along with our kids.

What do you see as the enticement of social media sites like Facebook, Snapchat, and Instagram? Social media is all about community, connectivity, affiliation, exhibition, and self-promotion. A 2015 report released by the Pew Research Center indicates 24 percent of teens are online almost constantly. To a great extent, access is facilitated by smartphones, with females accessing the internet via smartphones 75 percent of the time compared to laptops. The study indicated 92 percent of the teens go online daily, often several times a day.[7] Nearly 100 percent of teenagers in my present school are online throughout the day. (I say nearly, but I really don't know of one who doesn't have a phone or computer.) Regarding social media popularity, Snapchat is now in first place as the most actively used social media site among teens followed by Facebook, Instagram, Twitter, Pinterest, and Tumblr.[8] Add to this an average of 4,000 text messages sent per month, and that phone, to say the least, is a time-consuming device.[9]

What's so enticing about social media? Everything! One teen I spoke with noted that "social media is where life happens." Our kids live out a large part of their existence on these platforms. Reposts, retweets, and most importantly, likes are the social currency by which some teens gauge their worth. The more likes they have, the better they feel about themselves and their place in the social pecking order. In so many ways, kids expose their hearts—the best of what they believe about themselves—then ask, "Do you value me? If so, show me. Comment, like, forward my posts." Multiply this process by the mass quantity of sites they access, the forms of communication they use (video, photo, text, music, poetry, etc.), and one can begin to understand the composite of what a teen is projecting regarding who they are, what they believe about themselves, and hope others like about them.

If you want to know how your teen wants to be seen or thought of, look no further than their activity on social media. This is indeed the place where much of life is happening. A teen who is not allowed access to sites where most of their peers are playing and socializing is akin to being a leper, an outcast, a loner. Some parents would prefer this to the drama that results from social media. However, there is a place for balance, and there are some positives to be gained from it.

First, through social media, kids can stay connected to peers from all over the world. This connectivity has taken down geographic barriers that once isolated overseas families. Second, kids use social media the same way that we used the media of our day when we were teens—we just didn't have an online presence. They are trying on roles, sharing details about their political and social views, interests, and activities. Of course, the downside of this is they are doing these things online, which means what they share will be there forever. They are establishing a virtual footprint at a very young and vulnerable age.

How can we help our child understand the potential dangers of social media? Sadly, most teens lack the cerebral capacity to fully understand the long-term consequences of going on social rants, making political statements, or sending nude photos that *will* follow them the rest of their lives.

How do we get teens to envision how the actions they performed today will look like ten years from now...or even this weekend? Welcome to parenting adolescents. The challenge for parents is to continually remind, reinforce, and actively teach about appropriate online and offline behaviors. There should be no disconnect between the two. There are many examples in the media of individuals, companies, and countries that have had data exploited and publicly shared with the rest of the world. If it can happen to someone else, it can surely happen to your kids. I encourage parents to talk about what is socially acceptable when it comes to posting photos, comments, and other content *before* they allow their kids access to such sites. And by no means is this a one-off conversation. Such conversations are actively undertaken throughout the time your child is in the home. Use others' mistakes as examples; teach, actively monitor, and engage, engage, engage with the social media platforms your kids use. Specifically, make sure you are part of your child's social community. Whatever platforms they use, be sure they've accepted you into their circle—they've "friended" you—there. This will afford you the opportunity to monitor what they are doing online.

Each year, I meet with our ninth-grade students and speak on the issue of social media. Without exception, a large percentage of hands are raised when I ask the question, "Have you posted anything online you regret?" I wish I could pull back those regrets for them, but I can't. Neither can they. The question is, what will become of those comments, posts, pictures? Only time will tell.

Do colleges and universities monitor what kids do online as part of the college acceptance process? A 2016 survey from Cornerstone Reputation, an online reputation management company, found that 45 percent of admissions officers said they searched online for students who submitted applications, up from 36 percent just a year earlier. Also, just over two-thirds indicated they look up applicants on Facebook. By contrast, in 2012 only about 25 percent of admissions officers said they used Facebook and Google to vet applications.[10] You bet it matters what kids are doing online. I haven't yet heard of a student at my present school who has been denied admission to a particular university because of their activity on social media, but I fully anticipate this will happen.

17

Stressed Out

Stress is basically a disconnection from the earth,
a forgetting of the breath. Stress is an ignorant state.
It believes that everything is an emergency.
Nothing is that important.
Just lie down.

NATALIE GOLDBERG

The other morning, I received an alarming email. The subject heading read, *Emergency, please call!* My initial thought was that someone had died or was seriously injured. Fortunately, neither was the case.

The email was a plea from a distraught mother. Her eleventh-grade son, Andy, had had a terrible night. With papers, projects, sports practice, and exams the following day, this kid had more on his plate than he could handle. The stress was debilitating. Mom was worried something worse might result, prompting her clarion call for help.

Fortunately, the stress this young man was experiencing was not a common occurrence. Working with teachers, we postponed and removed some of his school tasks. This defused the anxiety for both him and his mom, but a new plan would be needed going forward. For some kids, however, stress and stress responses are the norm.

&.

The word *stress,* first coined by Hans Selye in 1936, was used to describe a nonspecific response of the body to any demand for change. Over the years, the term has expanded to include "a condition or feeling experienced when a person perceives that demands exceed the personal and social resources the individual is able to mobilize."[1] In its simplest form, stress is both a physiological and psychological response to some perceived or present danger.[2]

In school settings, stress can arise from a myriad of sources: prepping for an upcoming exam or presentation, meeting new people or friends, participating in musical or sporting events, or even dealing with the drama of social media. Perception fuels stress, and when left unchecked, it will metastasize. But what if stress didn't have to be an enemy? What if students learned to channel stress for positive outcomes? Nearly all the teens I work with who report pervasive and ongoing stress have little to poor time management and typically fit into one of two common patterns.

Stress Inducing Routine One

Teen comes home from school and sleeps three to five hours, eats dinner in their room (usually while watching a Net-flix series on laptop or phone), showers for about an hour, settles into work near 9:00 p.m., and eventually retreats to bed, phone in hand, sometime around 2:00 a.m....or whenever they feel like it.

Stress Inducing Routine Two

Teen comes home from school, sits behind their laptop a few hours, eats (usually under protest with family), retreats back to room, showers, continues doing "schoolwork" until parents enter room suggesting it's time for bed. (Parents have already made their presence known several times before this with little to no success.) Finally, around 11:00 p.m., parents insist, "It's time for bed!" at which point, student resists in the form of stress responses. Parents take computer, but teen protests that the smartphone must remain, as it serves as their alarm clock. They eventually get to bed sometime around 1:00 a.m.

These scenarios aren't presented—nor are they to be inter-preted—as bad kids making poor choices. My contention is quite the opposite: Without boundaries, technology isn't an aid to stress reduction; it is an impediment. With that in mind, I want to offer one suggestion that could significantly impact the level of stress kids experience. You've seen it before:

Have a set time for their computers and smartphones to come out of their room, regardless of their emotional state.

When your teen's competition for completing schoolwork is the World Wide Web, academics will lose out. And when this happens consistently, there will be excessive stress. I'm not so naive to believe this one step will reduce all stress, but it's a starting point.

Management and monitoring of child/adolescent technology are two pressing issues that many parents find difficult to address. But they shouldn't be dissuaded or discouraged from addressing them. On the contrary, they should be encouraged to know this is sometimes difficult work—that's a telltale sign that it is worth it.

If this resonates with what's occurring in your home, I encourage you to reach out to your child's counselor or school psychologist for support.

FAQs

Stress seems to be so much more common among teens than it was when we were teens. What's going on? No question, kids are reporting more stress than previous generations. Perhaps part of the answer is that we generalize and label many facets of life as stressful that were once considered normal parts of adolescence. For example, I have kids in my office on a frequent basis dealing with stress because they have two exams in one day or they've just broken up with a boyfriend/girlfriend or they're contending with parents who exasperate them.

While these issues are frustrating, they don't have to constitute ongoing and protracted stress...but they do. To be sure, mental health providers have become better at spotting the symptoms of anxiety/stress, but we've also created a culture that has normalized these responses. My argument for this is, boundaries are essential to regulating stress.

When was the last time you limited your child's options or activities in an effort to maintain balance? While kids can participate in numerous activities, attend extra help sessions, take multiple higher-level courses, take part in model UN, and travel on a multitude of exchanges, should they? Knowing the costs associated with each of these choices, at what point should parents enforce or establish boundaries as a hedge against stress?

The other day, I had a sixteen-year-old and her parents in my office. As a tenth grader, she was taking two advanced placement (AP) courses, and for the first time in her young life was experiencing the effects of the *cost* when taking accelerated courses. She was earning two Bs (the rest of her classes were As). As a result, she felt like a failure. The stress she and her folks were experiencing was palpable. This lovely kid was crushed by expectations she had placed on herself to be perfect, as measured by the previous A grades on her report card. She was sure her chances of attending an Ivy League school were dashed. "What's the use of going on," she wailed. Talk about life out of balance.

Far too often, kids and parents fail to count the cost of taking accelerated courses. For the record, advanced placement (AP), international baccalaureate (IB), or other accelerated courses in and of themselves aren't the cause of stress. Rather, it's the perception from both students and parents that kids can perform at high levels across all facets of their lives and somehow continue to keep life in balance. Typically, the first thing to give way is sleep. This exacerbates the onset of stress. Teens more often than not live in the moment. They need parents with perspective—parents who can see the bigger picture of and for their lives and, when needed, make course corrections to restore balance. Not only is this important in regard to academics but for extracurricular activities as well. And remember, this process can be aided by including other stakeholders (teachers, coaches, counselors) in a teen's life.

What if my child tells me they need more time on their computer, but I can tell it's contributing to their anxiety? I would agree to additional computer time under two conditions. First, look at their search history to see where they've been online for the past several hours/days/weeks. If they erase their search history or use a ghost screen, they are not being truthful. (When a student uses multiple screens to move back and forth between different types of application activity, they are using a "ghost screen." One screen, for example, may show school-related work, while the other will show social media, movies, and so on. To determine if they are doing this, swipe all four fingers across the trackpad from left to right when you view their computer. The four-finger sweep will reveal if the other screen is being utilized.)

Second, talk with their teachers. Ask them how much time, on average, is needed for the homework assigned. If the student truly does need more time, this should be provided. Many high school students report having three to three-and-a-half hours of homework each night; middle school students, one to one-and-a-half hours; and elementary students, fifteen minutes to an hour. Some international schools assign no homework other than reading, which is wonderful. Not all schools, however, adhere to this model. That being said, most teens I work with who report being consistently stressed also spend between two and four hours a night on social media, gaming, or watching shows.

What if my teen refuses to give up their computer or phone? Sadly, this does happen. If your teen refuses to comply, speak with your child's school counselor or the school psychologist. They can help create a plan to reinforce the structures you're attempting to establish. Schools can remove the computer from a student and even require them to turn in their smartphones to the office throughout the day. Counselors and psychologists can also partner with the teachers, informing them of the ongoing conflicts around technology. Finally, they will offer additional support to students and parents. Many schools have desktop computers that students can access while at school or will provide them with a notepad if they can't be trusted. The goal is to establish boundaries and balance and, at some point, to return the computer to them.

My teen tells me they need their phone to wake them up in the morning. How should I handle this? Purchase a clock radio! If you leave them with their smartphone, you've left them with total access to the internet in the palm of their hand. As I mentioned before, approximately 75 percent of females access the internet primarily through their smartphones, not laptop computers.[3]

What should I do when stress leads to panic attacks? I remember the first time a student came to my office in the throes of a panic attack. It was disturbing, perhaps even more for me than it was for the kid! I attempted to treat the physical manifestations, only to see things progressively get worse. My focus was in the wrong place. I needed to wait, allowing for her to process the physiological manifestations of the panic attack—namely, the cortisol and adrenalin. Once these chemicals are released into the bloodstream, it's difficult to have a rational conversation. When this is occurring, kids need a space out of range from the curious eyes of peers. They often rock back and forth, cry, or feel like they're having difficulty breathing. It can be very frightening for the kids. Fortunately, I've gained a good deal of understanding since then for helping kids get through panic attacks.

First, don't panic. I know—easier said than done. Recognize that a panic attack is a physiological response. No amount of patting on the back, stating everything will be okay, drinking water, or telling them to not think about the thoughts will mitigate the attack. Cortisol and adrenaline have been released by the body and will need to run their course. The typical panic attack lasts eight to twelve minutes.

For anyone—child or adult—to gain a footing with anxiety and panic, they have to be allowed to experience it. Distorted thinking (perception) fuels the anxiety and resulting panic. Distraction—rocking back and forth, listening to music, crying, drawing, scribbling, typing, or otherwise moving their hands and feet—offers a way to process the emotions. Give them the space and time to do so. Once they make it through the panic phase, they can begin to process the event.

One does not have to experience a panic attack personally to understand it, but it sure does wonders with kids when other people who have had similar experiences are able to share their story of how they made it through.

In the processing phase, help them work through the possible triggers. Sometimes kids can articulate what these are (class presentations, impending auditions or tryouts, peer meetings, etc.), sometimes they can't. Most of the time, a trigger originates in some form of misperception. The key is to identify the ideas, debunk or validate them, and then develop a plan of action to address them. This phase usually takes the longest, primarily because their thinking can be so distorted. Think of the process as untangling a giant knot. After they've spent a significant time tying up their thoughts, their thoughts must be lovingly challenged—or untied. Often, the processing phase runs simultaneously with the third phase—a return to a natural setting.

The most familiar natural setting in school is the classroom. Assuming the class is not a place of actual harm but of perceived harm, it is vital the student returns at some point. The repeated exposure (even with anxiety, minus the panic) is necessary to challenge and ultimately change the perception. When the student is allowed to go home, the anxiety may abate, but it has not been addressed.

Over time, kids develop strong pairing associations (when panicked, I flee; I don't want anxiety, so I'll stay home). These can become detrimental, especially in the long term. We want kids to be able to attend classes, to be in social situations, to feel anxiety but manage it. For many kids and parents with anxiety issues, these are frightening prospects. The flight response is at work in these situations. To counteract it, we must equip kids to challenge the perceptions, develop healthy coping skills, and face the challenges their perceptions present. It's heavy-lifting work, indeed.

Are there times when stress and anxiety are legitimate responses?
There certainly are. For example, some kids face daily bullying. If this isn't sorted out, either by them taking action or caring adults doing so, anxiety, including prolonged anxiety, will be an appropriate and expected response. The goal is for the anxiety to be channeled toward positive outcomes. It's also important to take into account that each child has a different threshold for anxiety and stress.

I feel like I'm being manipulated by my kid's stress episodes.
How can I manage, and help my child manage, these emotions?
You can avoid being manipulated by emotions by having
structure and predictability in place in the home. This makes it
much easier to understand what may or may not be emotional
manipulation. When pressures build up around schooling, for
example, do your kids start losing school items, give up on
homework, or become forgetful? If so, they may need more
expectations and routine, not less. Keep in mind, this takes time.
In my work with kids and families, I've found on average it
takes about twenty weeks of consistency to establish a new
pattern or habit. This number can seem unsettling, but routines
are both difficult to break and difficult to establish. Don't be
discouraged, however. I've seen many kids and parents walk
through this together, making necessary changes that resulted in
positive outcomes for the whole family.

What are your thoughts on helicopter parenting? A helicopter
parent is a parent who hovers, who takes an overprotective or
excessive interest in the life of their child or children.[4] It's not
uncommon for these children and teens to have parental
regulations well into their twenties because letting go is perhaps
more painful than hanging on. Helicopter parents give further
relevance to their lives by managing the affairs of their adult
children. Some pundits note this type of parenting is beneficial to
child and parent as it fosters community and connectivity.

My question to helicopter parents is as follows: At what age
or milestone should parents believe their children capable of
autonomy? Traditionally, this happens at age eighteen. In many
countries, that is considered the age of adulthood, when one is to
be treated and held accountable for their actions as an adult. The
legal demarcation remains, but control by helicopter parents has
prolonged the dependence of "adult children," extending juvenile
behaviors well into their twenties.

To state that this parenting style is wrong invokes a sub-
jective, perhaps cultural, bias. To state that we don't intend to
parent this way doesn't. Over the years, I've met quite a few
parents who hover. The intention is to be involved in their kids'
lives well into adulthood, including college choice, selection of a

major, where to live, and choice of a spouse. This is all under the pretense that they know what is best for their children.

Personally, I believe the ideal situation is that once our children reach adulthood (age eighteen), we can expect to continue to play a consultant role in kids' lives—but only when asked. For the rest of our lives, we will wait to be invited or will ask for permission to enter into the decisions our adult children are making. We hope we are provided opportunities to give wise counsel, but we will wait to be invited into them.

18

Can, Should, Cost:
Understanding Testing Accommodations
for AP/SAT/ACT

This is a test. It is only a test.
If this were your actual life,
You would be given better instructions.

MYRNA NEIMS

Email Subject: Requesting accommodations for testing

Email: Dear Dr. Devens, I know you don't know me, nor do you know our son, Richard. He will be a junior this year. For several years now, we have been concerned about his academic performance. This past summer, we had him tested and discovered he has attention deficit hyperactivity disorder (ADHD). We would like to request a time to meet with you to go over his evaluation and discuss accommodations. We would like to do this as soon as school begins in August, as he's scheduled to take the SAT in November. We're hoping he could have extra time for this exam. Kind Regards...

&

It has come to my attention over the years that parents sometimes start scheduling appointments with teachers and/or counselors around the time their child enters tenth grade (age fifteen or sixteen), expressing concerns regarding their teen's academic progress, when previously the child was not receiving any extra academic support. It isn't so much that their child is not doing well academically as it is the mounting concerns regarding the energy and effort being exerted to maintain their academic standing. Parents inquire what the school can do to help in the form of providing accommodations.

Why this grade; why this age? Why were their child's academic issues not noted by teachers, counselors, or learning support professionals throughout the last several years? The two most common explanations I've encountered are as follows:

- *Scenario 1.* An evaluation was completed sometime in elementary or primary school indicating learning concerns; however, since that time their child has not been utilizing or receiving any accommodations. The parents are now concerned their teen may be experiencing a resurgence of learning problems and won't be able to complete external exams (PSAT, SAT, AP, ACT, IB, etc.) without extended time.
- *Scenario 2.* External exams such as those noted above begin in the eleventh or twelfth grade. Kids and parents experience anxiety about not being able to complete exams because they run out of time. Knowing these exams contribute to the college admission process fuels their anxiety. Prior to this, there were no noted difficulties when taking timed exams.

The second example described Thomas. He had a cumulative GPA of 4.0 and had taken three AP courses (earning 5 out of 5 marks) without the aid of accommodations. Prior to his senior year, Thomas had not had any accommodations in any classes, nor did he have a history of learning issues. Nevertheless, a recent evaluation made by a licensed psychologist (without consulting the school regarding his academic progress) had indicated a discrepancy between his academic ability and his cognitive abilities. The evaluation had included parent and child interviews. The resulting diagnostic label (and the most common one ascribed to kids I work with) was attention deficit hyperactivity disorder (ADHD), primarily inattentive.

When I speak with other school psychologists, they also note ADHD is the most common issue they face in school settings. Racing to take the top spot, however, are anxiety disorders. I have seen a marked increase in anxiety-related issues over the past five years—so much so that I am confident it is tied to online/social media use. I have seen hints of this in professional literature, but nothing conclusive to date. Anecdotally, I do think there is a strong link. I predict the research will begin to support this in the next few years.

In both scenarios above, parents emphasize that their child is spending increasing amounts of time completing school tasks, working with tutors, and pulling away from extracurricular activities, all to maintain their academic standing. Parents question if there is a disability or if the diagnosis their child received several years earlier is somehow the cause of the present learning difficulties. These are reasonable questions. I would seek guidance, too, if one of my kids performed well for so many years and then, suddenly or over the course of several months, began performing at lower levels.

When I'm presented with such situations, I discuss three key terms with the parents and student: *can, should,* and *cost.*

Teens and parents often fail to take into account the *cost* of taking advanced courses. It's assumed that if a teen takes advanced courses, they can handle the rigor, time management, and emotional regulation when pressures mount. Difficulty can arise when motivation, maturation, emotions, peer influences, genetics, parental guidance/support, and a host of other variables interact, influencing the rate of learning. It's not that the student can't learn or that they aren't smart. Rather, it's that those involved have failed to take into account the potential costs associated with these courses, including increased anxiety, stress, sleep deprivation, and a lack of emotional regulation.

Can a teen essentially have it all? Yes—for a while. As time wears on, however, cracks begin to form. The weight and volume of pressure build and eventually become more than they can handle. This results in a deluge of emotional outpouring. It's important to reemphasize that, in most cases, the issue isn't a teen's intelligence. Rather, it's about balance (time management, emotional regulation, organization, etc.). The essential question is whether a teen should take as many advanced courses as possible or be involved in so many extracurricular activities, given the cost?

When speaking with parents about *can, should,* and *cost,* I provide them with a worksheet like the one in Figure A. I instruct them to place a checkmark on the line where they believe their child's ability is for each category. The lower the mark on the scale, the more difficulties noted. The higher the score, the fewer difficulties noted. If scores are markedly lower in some domains, those are the areas we focus on to create plans for support.

Figure A

Cognitive ability:

Low _____High

Emotional regulation:

Low _____High

Organization:

Low _____High

Time management:

Low _____High

Sleep:

Low _____High

Stress management:

Low _____High

I also have the teen complete the same scale. It is not uncommon for kids and parents to have slightly different or even markedly different perceptions of how the teen manages each domain. This is to be expected and makes for some great conversations as to why and how each perceives the teen's ability to either regulate well or not so well. The point of this activity is to open dialogue and prepare ahead of time for what-if situations.

The collected information provides for rich discussions as parents and kids consider future courses and extracurricular commitments, as well as possible support options. For example, if parents and their student note high cognitive abilities and organization skills but poor emotional regulation and sleep management, I will suggest the student not take too many advanced courses until they demonstrate they have these weaker areas sorted. (Sadly, this advice often falls on deaf ears.) The suggestion might also include having parents establish a set time each evening for all technology to be out of their teen's room. With this rule in place, how does the teen respond? Are they bucking this or acting out emotionally? Are they getting the necessary sleep to function during the day? If an appropriately balanced schedule is kept consistently by the teen through grade ten (ages fifteen or sixteen), it's a good indication they are ready for additional challenges.

RESPONSE TO INTERVENTION (RTI)

A school's primary responsibility is to help its students maximize their learning potential. While learning is a primary objective in a school setting, however, it is not the sole objective. Schools make concerted efforts to develop the whole child—their academic, social, emotional, and physical well-being. If difficulties impede a child's development, schools take proactive measures to support him or her. In recent years this process has been termed *Response to Intervention* (RTI).

RTI is a multi-tiered approach designed to help all students learn at higher levels. A student's academic, emotional, and social progress is monitored over the years to determine the need for additional research-based instructional support. If necessary, students are provided with specific interventions at increasing levels of intensity to support learning, coping, and emotional regulation. Progress is closely monitored to assess learning rates and outcomes.

As a starting point, and in theory, all students are provided with high-quality classroom instruction. Nearly 90 percent of learning and behavioral/social-emotional issues are sorted by implementing strategies and interventions in the regular classroom setting. This may include one-on-one or small group instruction, study sessions during lunch, during breaks, or after school, providing handouts, working with peers, additional time, and ongoing student assessments that target specific areas of weakness. Also, counseling support may be provided to assist the child and parents with emotional regulation and parenting concerns.

If the above interventions are unsuccessful, additional steps may be taken. These would include enrolling the student in a learning support class where there is further, targeted instruction, undertaking psychoeducational assessments highlighting specific areas of weakness, and providing targeted interventions and establishing a plan that highlights various accommodations the teacher can use in classroom settings.

If the student qualifies as having a learning disability, they may be eligible to apply for external testing accommodations through organizations such as the College Board (AP, SAT) and ACT; however, these organizations have specific criteria to qualify. Schools do not determine these standards. While accommodations can be provided in schools to help students with academic, social, and emotional needs, these aren't extended to external organizations (SAT, AP, IB, ACT). To qualify, each case (student) is presented to these agencies, and they make the decision for accommodation based on their predetermined criteria.

The RTI process varies from school to school. Some schools require psychoeducational testing prior to granting student supports; other schools focus on functionality (what the student is doing or not doing) to determine eligibility for services. Each school sets their own criteria.

UNDERSTANDING THE TESTING ACCOMMODATION PROCESS

There are several questions used to determine eligibility for College Board and ACT special testing accommodations. In my role as a school psychologist, I relay this information to the parents, then add any additional information (functional data) that I have gathered over the years regarding their child's progress. I will list these questions below and present what I've learned over the years to help clarify.

1. **Is the student presently using the accommodations they are requesting?**

    It does not matter to the College Board or ACT if a child has a diagnosed disability as sole criteria for determining eligibility for accommodations. In fact, if the statement, "my child was assessed six years ago and has a diagnosis of attention deficit disorder–inattentive" is the only evidence put forth, the accommodation would not be provided. The College Board notes: "A diagnosis, in and of itself, does not necessitate testing accommodations without evidence the disabling condition leads to a functional impairment [and] limits a child's ability to take College Board exams."[1] This criterion holds true for AP tests as well as ACT, PSAT, and SAT.

2. **Has the student been using accommodations for a minimum of four months?**

    The four-month window doesn't include summer holidays or other breaks. Teachers will be asked to provide evidence of a student's assessment difficulties with and without the aid of accommodations: "How or in what ways is the use of the accommodation effective?" This information is of high importance to these organizations, as they will review teacher comments as part of the process for determining eligibility.

    Day-to-day, historical progress is also critical in the decision-making process. The term used to describe this is *functional progress.* A summary of past learning, including grades, grade point average, individual awards/recognition, current classes, as well as outside supports, must be summarized and included in the application. Also, any standardized assessments a student has completed in years past may be requested.

    Functionality drives the entire accommodations process. There must be a history of consistent academic problems, use of support services, or of needing formal accommodations in a school setting.

3. **For accommodations based on learning issues, does the student have a current psychoeducational evaluation, including a cognitive and achievement measure? Have these assessments been undertaken within the last five years for the College Board (or three years for the ACT)?**

An evaluation by a physician, social worker, or mental health provider, without a cognitive and achievement measure, would not be justification for accommodations. For example, if a physician noted a child has ADHD but didn't order a cognitive and achievement measure, the student would not be granted accommodations based on this alone. The physician may have had rating scales that parents, teachers, and the child completed, or some other assessments given; but without a cognitive and achievement measure, the College Board and ACT will, in nearly all cases, reject the request for accommodation. If a case is presented that describes deficits in learning, metrics (such as the ones below) should be included in the application.

Common Names of Cognitive Measures:
- Wechsler Adult Intelligence Scale (WAIS)
- Wechsler Intelligence Scale for Children (WISC)
- Woodcock-Johnson Psychoeducational Battery-Revised Tests of Cognitive Abilities
- Stanford-Binet Intelligence Scales (SBS)
- Kaufman Adolescent and Adult Intelligence
- Kaufman Assessment Battery for Children (KABC)
- Differential Ability Scale (DAS)

Common Names of Achievement Measures:
- Woodcock-Johnson: Test of Achievement
- Scholastic Abilities Test for Adults (SATA)
- Stanford Diagnostic Reading Tests (SDRT)
- Wechsler Individual Achievement Test (WIAT)
- Kaufman Test of Educational Achievement (KTEA)
- Gates-MacGintie Reading Tests (GMRT)
- Test of Written Language (TOWL)
- Kaufman Test of Educational Achievement (KTEA)

4. Does the student have a diagnosed disability?

Is there formal testing administered by a trained professional (school psychologist or clinical psychologist) using sound psychometrics and indicating specific areas of weakness? Does it provide a diagnosis? The diagnosis should include information regarding types of accommodations to be utilized for supporting learning.

5. Does the student have an accommodation plan, 504, Individual Education Plan (IEP), or another plan of support that has been active for more than one academic year?

The child in question must have some formal learning plan in place describing the types of accommodations afforded. This plan typically includes a brief history highlighting the learning issues, assessments undertaken, functional data from teachers describing day-to-day difficulties, and present services provided. Also, this document should include information related to when services began, what outcomes are expected, and what accommodations are provided. Lastly, some standardized measures (assessments) should be provided, demonstrating that the accommodations have been helpful in supporting the student's learning.

FAQs

What if my child has a mental health issue that impacts their learning and results in the need for accommodations? In cases where mental health issues necessitate the need for accommodations, a psychological report must be submitted to the College Board or ACT for review. This report should include an in-depth explanation describing how the student's mental health issues impact learning and, thus, the need for accommodations. Based on information from teachers describing functional limitations, along with a psychological report, a determination will be made regarding use of accommodations for external assessments.

What if the issue necessitating the need for accommodations is neither mental health nor learning but medical? The student would need a medical report that supports the need for the requested accommodations. For example, if vision issues prevent the student from working with twelve-point font (typical reading size print) and they require large print test books for exams, as well as additional time, these requests must be substantiated with medical documentation. Also, school testing records should support the use of these accommodations, unless the issue is a recent (last four months) medical occurrence. Further, the accommodations provided should be noted in the school accommodation plan for the student. For instance, I worked with a student who required a scribe and double time due to their medical condition.

A half-page, scribbled note from a physician (yep, I've received these) will not suffice. Documentation outlining specific medical conditions, along with metrics (medically recognized measurement assessments) is needed when presenting medical accommodation requests. Psychoeducational assessments would not be necessary for a medical request like my example, as visual impairment is not a learning issue. Sometimes, however, both medical and psychological issues are present. Each case is unique, but evidence must support both cases.

My child is working with a tutor two nights a week, frequently staying up past midnight doing homework, and does more on weekends and over vacations. I am worried they are not going to do well on the upcoming PSAT/SAT/AP exams. They are working as hard as they can but are still not able to complete their exams on time. This is causing great amounts of stress and may impact what colleges they can attend. Can you please help? The scenario above is among the most common I deal with when it comes to the subject of accommodations and kids without a history of learning issues. I note the following observations with increasing concern.

Many kids are pushing themselves to the breaking point. Parents and kids are exhausted and want help. They ask me—believing I hold sway with these external agencies—to allow extended time. The reality is, I can't. I don't make these decisions. The College Board and ACT have set criteria for what constitutes a learning issue and merits accommodations. No amount of status, titles, outside tutor support, stress related to academic load, or even records stating "exams were not completed on time" will matter when determining eligibility. My charge as a school counselor/psychologist (or whoever coordinates these services in the school your child attends) is to function as a go-between with these external agencies. I collect the necessary documentation and pass it on for them to make the determination for accommodations. It's all about their criteria.

In noting the above, I'm not trying to be callous, cavalier, or nonchalant. My heart breaks when I hear kids report their struggles. Sadly, some of this stress is self- or parent-imposed. Kids and parents can't have everything they want when it comes to learning. There *will* be costs. The questions I ask parents and kids are as follows: Did you or your child think about the costs before signing up for courses and extracurricular commitments? Did you and your child reflect on the previous year and how the academic stresses were handled before signing on for classes the following year?

Our responsibility as parents is to encourage, support, and yes, even at times, to say no to our kids when life gets out of balance. Key indicators that kids need help regaining balance include reduction in sleep under the pretense of keeping up with classes, lack of emotional regulation (usually happens during exam weeks or around major project deadlines), inability to interact with family around traditional family times (such as supper, vacations, attending worship), and disregarding relationships.

19

Why Alcohol and Teens Don't Mix

*Almost anything can be preserved in alcohol,
except health, happiness, and money.*

MARY WILSON LITTLE

"What happened?" A bewildered, seventeen-year-old Adam asked himself this question out loud as he sat in my office, fumbling for words to describe the previous weekend's events.

"The last thing I remember before passing out...I was with my friends outside the dance club. I woke up the next morning in an alley with a sore jaw, and fractured ribs. I was covered in vomit. I figured it was time to talk to someone about my alcohol use."

Sadly, this wasn't our first conversation about alcohol, nor would it be our last.

It turns out Adam's friends ditched him, figuring they would be in trouble if they returned him home in a drunken state. As far as he could surmise, after his friends left him, some thugs jumped him, stole his wallet, and left him with a few parting kicks to his midsection.

ॐ

I've often wondered what happened to Adam. He has since graduated and his family moved on to another post. Knowing what I know about adolescent alcohol use, I'm certain this wasn't his last incident. Adam's story doesn't reflect most of the kids I work with, but it does speak to a continued concern I have regarding the self-reported use of alcohol (what kids share openly via surveys) among international teens.

Adolescence brings on a host of new social and emotional experiences, and these experiences stretch teens to the limit, especially when it comes to developing healthy coping mechanisms.

WHY TEENS DRINK

When I ask kids why they drink, the most commonly noted responses are to have fun, to unwind, to lower inhibitions, to blow off steam, to relax, to feel good, and to fit in. Essentially, they believe that they must put a drug into their bodies—one that fundamentally alters the way their brains function—before they can have fun. To justify their need or right to drink, teens resort to (faulty) perceptions such as, "Everyone is drinking, so it's not a big deal." For the past eight years and as part of our alcohol awareness initiatives at the school where I am employed, I've been anonymously surveying students. One of the questions I ask is, "What percentage of your peers do you think has consumed alcohol during the past thirty days?" Interestingly, throughout all the years of collecting responses to this question, the student estimations have not squared with reality. Depending on their year in school (freshman, sophomore, junior, senior), students tend to overestimate 20 to 50 percent, with freshmen distorting reality the most. Because perceptions form reality, this is vital information for teens, parents, and educators to understand. Unless we challenge perceptions, success at changing reality will be marginal at best.

When alcohol becomes a consistent part of a teen's developmental process, strong pairing associations can occur that may result in unhealthy patterns and choices of behavior. These associations include *fun=alcohol*, *stress=alcohol*, or *lower inhibitions=alcohol*. Over time, these patterns form the basis of habits; however, this formula cannot be distilled to the simplistic equation *response=behavior*, because alcohol has biochemical properties.

Alcohol contains a chemical known as *ethyl alcohol*. This drug is absorbed into the bloodstream through the lining of the stomach and carried to the central nervous system, where it acts to depress or slow functioning by binding to various neurons. While most other drugs have specific receptors they bind to in the brain, alcohol does not. This means alcohol affects each of us in slightly different ways. Typically, it first depresses (turns off) areas of the brain controlling judgment and inhibition—arguably two things teens need the most. As more alcohol is consumed, it depresses other parts of the central nervous system. The chemicals in alcohol attach themselves to brain-cell receptors and, over time, replace or alter the body's natural chemicals. It's a little like using leaded fuel in a car designed for unleaded—it will get you home, but over time, it will ruin vital car parts.

Sadly, some parents willingly provide alcohol to teens (pay-parties) or allow their teens to drink, accepting the mantra: "Kids are going to drink, so we might as well teach them to do so responsibly." Parents taking this faulty line of reasoning need to understand that alcohol consumption doesn't foster responsible behavior, it suppresses it! Parents may be contributing to alcohol-related issues for their children well into adulthood. Results from the National Longitudinal Epidemiologic Survey of 27,616 American youth showed that the lifetime alcohol dependence rates of kids who initiated alcohol use by age fourteen were four times as high as those who started at age twenty or older.[1] These are sobering statistics.

Why do we have laws regulating the use of alcohol among adolescents? Our hope as a society and culture is that teenagers will learn to cope with life's hurts, joys, trials, and socially awkward moments without relying on a drug to bridge the gaps. It is presumed that, by the time a person reaches the age of eighteen or twenty-one, they have gone through enough life experiences without the aid of alcohol that they can be responsible regarding their alcohol use. Remember, alcohol use among teens is primarily about coping.

Alcohol may be prevalent in our culture, but it doesn't have to be a part of our students' lives. The more parents and mentors stay involved by asking questions, speaking with other parents, and keeping dialogue open, the greater the likelihood teens will grow into more mature adults who make healthy choices.

FAQs

International families are exposed to various cultures where alcohol is prevalent, and teens seem to be able to cope with this better than kids back in the United States. Why do we make this such a big issue? Arguments are frequently made by parents who justify the use of alcohol for their teen by saying, "Alcohol is an embedded part of our culture. We see no problem with our teen drinking." Alcohol may be a cultural practice, yes, but that doesn't justify its use. Delaying alcohol use fosters healthy social and emotional maturation. Consuming alcohol stifles this process.

Another common parental justification for teenage alcohol use is, "My teen is going to drink at some point anyway, so why not teach them how to do this responsibly?" Folks, this is just nutty logic (which is an acceptable psychological term to describe faulty parenting rationale). Alcohol is a central nervous system suppressant. When teens drink, they lose the ability to think responsibly—regardless of whether they drink at a club or at home with you monitoring their consumption. Physiologically, alcohol works the same way regardless of who is serving it. Your teenagers need all the mental faculties they can muster to think responsibly without putting a drug like alcohol into their bodies. Now is not the time to encourage alcohol consumption.

Another faulty perception shared by some parents is, "If we don't teach kids to drink responsibly, they will go off the deep end when they get to university." The kids who go off the deep end at college are the same ones who do so as teens. Going off to college doesn't transform one into a binge drinker. Remember, drinking is about coping. Kids who use alcohol to cope in high school are also the ones who use it to cope in college and beyond. Yes, there are exceptions to that rule, but your child isn't likely one of them.

It seems like many of my teen's friends are drinking, but my daughter tells me she doesn't. Can I still trust her to be in an environment where peers and alcohol are present? Sadly, a reality facing many teens is the presence of alcohol at social gatherings. The issue isn't so much about trusting your daughter; it's about dealing with temptations, pressures, and possibilities in an environment where peers are drinking. While you may be able to fully trust your daughter, there are other forces at work that could tip the scale in favor of her drinking. This doesn't mean she violated your trust as much as it demonstrates her inability to withstand temptation—and I don't fault her for this. Neither kids nor adults are meant to be placed in settings where temptations are present and then be expected to continually resist them. It's about avoiding these tempting situations altogether.

If your teen is hanging with kids who are drinking on a regular basis and he/she has no social support from other peers who aren't drinking, he/she most likely *will* succumb to experimentation. The key is having positive peer influences supporting positive life choices. I believe it's possible for teens to go through high school and not drink. I know it is. I was one of those kids. This wasn't so much about taking the higher moral ground or religious objections as it was about witnessing the devastating effects of alcohol in the community. Added to this, I had great high school friends (thanks, Nate and Keenan) who also made the choice not to drink. Together we supported one another through the challenges we encountered.

We just found out our ninth-grader (age fourteen) has been drinking with his friends. What should we do? Knowing that alcohol use is about coping and that your son has begun experimentation with alcohol at such an early age, I would be concerned. I would want to better understand the context for his drinking. For example, some kids drink because they want to de-stress, fit in, or have fun. What are the underlying reasons for your teen's alcohol use?

Long gone are the days when you could self-select friends for your teen; however, there are organizations, clubs, and groups that your child could be a part of that can provide positive influences. I would also look to other caring adults in the community who could provide support. I've worked with a few families who make it a point to provide summer opportunities for their kids to be in positive-influencing environments during a portion of the summer. This might include Outward Bound experiences, attending summer camp, working, or other activities where the possibility of substance use is diminished. In the immediate, I encourage you to partner with your teen's school (teachers, coaches, counselors), forming a stronger partnership of support for your child. Depending on the level of substance use and peer influences, I would also consider seeking professional counseling support.

What advice about drugs would you offer to parents of preteens? I appreciate questions like this. They are a reminder that parents are being proactive, not waiting for issues to arise but addressing them before they do. Regarding alcohol use, I suggest having conversations with the kids early and often. Make clear your position on alcohol consumption. For example, in our home we find naturally occurring opportunities (media, events at school, etc.) where teens have consumed alcohol or other drugs and went on to make poor decisions. It might be a car accident, others being harmed, or doing foolish things while under the influence that become topics of discussion between us and our children. When these talks occur, we reiterate our position on alcohol and drug use.

At the publishing of this book, our children are ages twelve and eight. They have yet to be exposed to the peer/cultural pressures of substance use. Regardless, we want them to understand what these drugs are, why kids take them, and (at an age-appropriate level), what happens when kids consume them. As they move into adolescence, we will continue these conversations at deeper levels. In essence, we're being intentional. We understand fully that our kids, like yours, will be in social situations where they will have to make a choice regarding substance use. In those moments, our hope is that they will pause and remember the innumerable conversations we've had over the years regarding substance use, our beliefs, and their character.

At a parent gathering where we discussed alcohol use, one of our deputy principals shared with us the following helpful suggestions when discussing the issue of alcohol use with our teens.

- Be explicit about your alcohol and drug expectations, rules, and consequences.
- Share medical (physiological) information about alcohol

and drugs with your child.

- Wait up for your child and give the "hug-and-sniff test."
- Be your child's "out" so they can say, "No thanks, my parents will kill me if they smell alcohol on my breath."
- Encourage your child to delay their first encounter with alcohol. If your child protests, saying "everyone else is allowed to drink," he or she might be hanging out with drinkers.
- If you think your child is going to clubs or purchasing alcohol, check his/her wallet for a fake ID.
- Monitor your child's social media and check what their friends are posting.

20

Know the Signs of Suicide

Sometimes even to live is an act of courage.

SENECA

After sixteen years in Nebraska, Kevin's dad, a petrochemical engineer, accepted a job in Saudi Arabia, some 7,000 plus miles away from Runza sandwiches and Big Red football. Kevin, a self-described introvert, found that the geographical and cultural isolation of Saudi didn't offer much to draw him out. To mitigate feelings of hopelessness and despair, he resorted to drinking—excessively. Also, Kevin began skipping classes and school altogether, electing to sleep off his hangovers. Four months into his first year in Saudi Arabia, he began expressing a desire to self-harm. Kevin's goal wasn't to end his life as much as it was to stop the psychological pain.

"I felt hopeless and helpless. Hurting myself was the only out I could think of to end the pain. I was a messed-up kid. As a twenty-five-year-old, I look back on that time and recognize that I needed help; I needed hope. I'm glad my parents got me the help I needed—it's made all the difference."

❧

FACTS AND FIGURES

Suicide is the third leading cause of death among persons ages ten to fourteen; second among persons ages fifteen to twenty-four.[1] It's estimated that, for every youth who dies by suicide, as many as two hundred attempt it.[2] For every three students who attempt suicide, only one receives medical attention. Of the reported suicides in the ten to twenty-four age group,

81 percent of the deaths were male, and 19 percent were female.[3] Adolescent females are one-and-a-half to two times more likely than adolescent males to have thought about and attempted suicide, while adolescent males are four to five times more likely than adolescent females to complete a suicide.[4] Adolescent females die in approximately one out of twenty-five attempts; males, one out of three attempts. These differences are attributed to the methods of lethality.[5] In nearly three-quarters of suicide attempts, a person has a mental health issue (depression, anxiety, eating disorder, etc.).[6] Lastly, those who have attempted suicide are up to six times more likely to attempt again than adolescents who have not attempted suicide.[7]

As disconcerting as these facts and figures are, it is of utmost importance that parents are aware of their child's wellbeing and safety. Surprisingly, research indicates one-half to three-quarters of parents were unaware of their child's suicidal thinking.[8] Other studies note parents were unaware of their children's depressive symptoms and alcohol use, both risk factors associated with suicidal behavior.[9] This raises the questions: When should a parent be concerned their child may be suicidal? What actions should they take?

KNOW THE SIGNS

Immediate Warning Signs
Seek help immediately...
- when a child is threatening to hurt or harm themselves;
- when a child has a plan to harm, is seeking access, and preparing to carry it out;
- if there have been previous attempts at self-harm; or
- when someone writes or talks about suicide based on some perceived or real trauma.

Risk Factors
Consult with your child's counselor or other outside mental health professional if your child manifests one or more of the following signs. While alone these are not imminent indicators of self-harm, a number of these together do indicate the need for further investigation and support.

Protracted (long-lasting) feelings of:

- depression, anxiety, eating issues
- hopelessness
- rage
- anger
- revenge
- reckless or risky behavior
- expressions of feeling trapped
- increased drug/alcohol use
- withdrawal from family/friends

Protective Factors:
The following protective factors correlate with positive adolescent social-emotional growth. The more factors noted, the less likely a child is to engage in self-harming thoughts or actions.

- family and school connectedness
- available outlets for kids to ask for help
- helping kids identify trusted adults
- available outlets and opportunities to demonstrate competence beyond academics
- positive/consistent academic growth and achievement
- positive self-esteem and coping skills
- access to and care for mental, physical, or substance issues

The National Longitudinal Study on Adolescent Health surveyed more than 90,000 students in grades nine through twelve (ages thirteen through eighteen) and found a student's feeling of connectedness was the *number one* protective factor against suicidal behavior.[10] More specifically, kids who believed teachers treated them fairly, who formed supportive relationships with peers, and who felt like they were part of a school were less likely to engage in at-risk behaviors, including suicide. Therefore, when discussing this topic with students, our focus is on education, prevention, and living.

A GOOD PLACE TO START

If you have questions regarding your child's social and emotional heath, a good place to start is by speaking with their teachers, coaches, counselors, and other mentors. They can provide insights into your student's thinking and behaviors. Think of this as providing layers of support in the lives of kids. The more contact points, the healthier the child.

Lastly, if you suspect your child is thinking of self-harm, trust your instincts, act, and seek support.

FAQs

We moved overseas six months ago. Our son is now struggling academically and socially. What should we do? It's not uncommon for kids to experience adjustment issues moving abroad, but there is a point when parents should become concerned. If you note your child/teen is pulling away from activities they once enjoyed (clubs, sports, music, etc.) or if you observe a drop in academic performance, become concerned that they are resorting to unhealthy coping behaviors (drinking/drug use), or there are changes in sleep and eating habits, I would seek help. This may include speaking with your child's counselor, teachers, coaches, or other caring adults within the school and/or community. The above are telltale signs of concern, commonly associated with depression.

My teen is cutting on her arms and legs. Why is she doing this? This is a frequent question from parents who are concerned their child may be suicidal. When kids engage in self-injury (cutting), the goal isn't suicide. It is pain regulation. Kids are trying to express physically something they feel emotionally. I'm not mitigating the behavior (self-injury) and am very concerned when a young person has a pain in their heart so deep that they must attempt to work it out physically, but in most cases, this isn't a sign that a student is suicidal.

If your child is cutting on their arms, legs, thighs, stomach, or elsewhere, try to find the underlying issues. Most kids who self-injure are physically expressing a psychological issue pertaining to their worth, purpose, or life's meaning. These are the areas of exploration I would consider.

An important side note is that, in some cases, the self-injurious behaviors may be attributed to previous or ongoing physical or sexual abuse.[11] If you observe a child (especially one under age twelve) engaging in self-injury actions, consultation with a psychologist or medical provider is a must.

What role does social media play in suicide? Many kids use social media as a means of garnering worth, purpose, and meaning. How much this contributes to feelings of depression varies from person to person, but comparing what others have to what one does not have can intensify the emotion. Teens use social media to project something of themselves regarding how they want others to think of them. Social media is about self-expression. For example, an article written for Netsanity reported that "every year teens spend a total of seven full work days taking selfies."[12] What message are they attempting to convey? For some, it's the likes they receive from their postings that become a barometer of their worth. If kids are using social media to determine if they are good, pretty, sporty, skinny, or funny enough, this can certainly contribute to depression. Stating that social media in a vacuum causes teens to commit suicide would be an oversimplification. Most often, it is just one of many possible factors.

If your child is spending an increasing amount of time on social media and manifests increasing anxiety when access is restricted, it's a good sign they will need your help.

My daughter's friend has expressed to her thoughts of harming herself, but she has asked her not to tell anyone. As you can imagine, this has caused considerable anxiety for my daughter. What should she do? When teens reach out for help, I'm encouraged. I am encouraged because they recognize what *healthy* looks like. I am encouraged because they are willing to risk a friendship to potentially save a life. And I am encouraged because they see a better tomorrow, one their friend can't see in the present. Each year, I have conversations like the one this mom noted regarding a friend who was thinking of harming herself. In most cases, two or more caring friends meet with me to discuss concerns regarding a peer's wellbeing. First, I express my gratitude that they are good friends to this person and want to reach out for help. Second, I unpack what this might entail. In most cases, kids ask if it's possible for them not to be identified as ratting out their friend. In many cases, this simply isn't possible. Kids are intuitive and talkative; the information will get back to them as to who told. The fear for the concerned friend is twofold: Their friend will get in trouble (parents will find out) and/or their breach of trust (in telling me) will harm their friendship. In both cases, I acknowledge these realities, but I also offer a way to deal with these concerns.

When a student expresses a desire to harm themselves, they are not thinking in healthy ways. In many cases, they are dealing with a disorder (depression, anxiety, etc.) that's contributing to feelings of despair and suicidal ideation.[13] The concerned friends must understand that their friend isn't well and is attempting to reach out for help by telling them. Second, and this is a difficult realization, they may have to lose a friendship in order save a life. When I tell kids this, tears often follow. They realize the weight of what they are about to do—reveal the name of their hurting friend. It is at this point that some kids back away. They don't want to risk the friendship, even if it means their friend harms themselves. Most kids, however, do share their friend's name.

Once provided, I schedule a meeting with the student (in most cases, I walk over to their classroom and get them) as soon as possible. I discuss with them the concerns that have been raised and assess their level of suicide intentionality—all enveloped in love, support, and care. Kids respond in a thousand different ways. Some open up, sharing the hurt in their heart; others become defensive, denying the allegations. They are often angry. They feel betrayed by the friend they thought they could trust.

As I speak with them, I know full well they are trying to figure out who told me. I do address this with them, attempting to help them understand the purpose of our meeting isn't about getting them in trouble with their parents. The angry kids in most cases don't want their parents to know what's going on, mostly because they attribute the psychological pain they are experiencing to their parents. These are difficult cases. I know I will have to bring parents into the conversation. If parents are part of the problem, we need to address it.

What's the connection between depression and suicide? It is estimated that 15 percent of those who are clinically depressed die by suicide.[14] Depression is a complex disorder that clouds a teen's ability to think clearly, to see a better future, or to have the resolve (physically or psychologically) to make a change. Teenagers who are depressed and talk about committing suicide—saying things like, "I'd be better off dead," writing stories and poems about death, engaging in reckless behavior, giving away prized possessions, or medicating with alcohol and drugs (other than prescribed)—need help. If you suspect a depressed teen is suicidal, take immediate action. Parents must keep a focus on seeking their child's physical safety. This may include seeking residential treatment. Far too many times I've had parents comment, "Something in my gut indicated there was a problem." You have been given parental intuition—trust it.

21

A Letter to Husbands

*The most important thing
a father can do for his children
is to love their mother.*

THEODORE M. HESBURGH

When I was a kid, I enjoyed watching Westerns—those gun-slinging cowboys who bravely faced the cold, the cruel, and the cantankerous. What they lacked in words, they made up for with action, electing their six-shooter to be their spokesman. They provided a generation of boys—who would one day become men—a template for responding to people and problems: When wronged, make it right; when faced with difficult circumstances, persevere; fight for the underdog; stand for justice; and most importantly, be honorable in both word and deed.

Fast-forward to 2018. The media's image of fathers has changed markedly. Instead of being shown as courageous, supportive, and devoted, today's men are portrayed as spineless, noncommittal, and impulsive. In short, Hollywood has not been kind to us, and perhaps with some due level of criticism. While most men may not be in positions of influence to change the media's perception of what it means to be a father, we can certainly make a difference in a far more significant arena—our own home.

&

In my work as a psychologist, I've noted with increasing concern a common pattern of choices that men make over time—choices that erode the relationships most important in their lives, namely those with their spouse/partner and children. These choices include seeking intimacy outside of marriage, placing career aspirations above family, and lacking significant friendships with other males.

Let me say from the start, writing a chapter of this nature is a difficult undertaking. Doing so runs the risk of readers assuming these issues don't apply to me or that I'm casting aspersions. This is simply not so. I am a husband and father; I'm made of the same stuff as every other guy. The words I write aren't moral platitudes for readers—they apply to my life as well.

Let me also say, some readers may object to a chapter devoted to this subject, assuming I don't believe it applies to women as well. Well, it does. That being said, however, based on the work I engage in, I primarily see the outworking of these issues in respect to men. This happens primarily for three reasons.

Men Seeking Intimacy Outside of Marriage

Sexual acts, whether adultery or other degrees of sexual gratification, outside of the marital relationship will exact a significant cost on the person and the family. There is no free sexual exploration. What we do in private matters! It matters to our wives; it matters to our kids. In media culture, the slogan, "If it feels good do it," is the mantra of the day; however, sex is more than a physical act. It also contains moral and emotional significance.

Sex unites a husband and wife on an emotional and intimate level, but any sex has the same power. A person who has been united sexually with his or her spouse and then unites with someone else adulterates that relationship, hence the term *adultery*. Adultery introduces an element of *dis*-integrity to a relationship formerly integrated, whole, and pure. When a husband engages in sexual activities with someone or something (pornography), damage is done to the whole person. This activity cannot be compartmentalized. Involvement in sexual activities outside of the marital relationship debilitates the relationship, often leaving a person intimacy impaired.

For the record, no one falls into adultery (including pornography); rather, this is a gradual process. As a person begins this descent, they go to great lengths to rationalize the activities they engage in. Over time, there exists such intimacy erosion that significant damage is done to the marital relationship, quite often resulting in a disintegration of the marriage.

Humans are designed for intimacy; sex either fosters this or spoils it. What deliberate steps are we taking to protect our marriages? With divorce figures at or above 50 percent, how we answer this question may determine which side of the divorce rate our marriages end up on.

Placing Career Aspirations above Family

We men are *big* fans of titles—CEO, CFO, president, vice-president, and so on. However, the most important titles we will be remembered for are those of *husband, father,* and *friend.*

Recently, while teaching a psychology course, I asked my eleventh- and twelfth-grade students to complete the following sentence: "My father _____." Nearly one third of the kids' comments reflected their father's work ("My father travels often," "My father works long hours," or "My father's work is important"). The purpose of noting this isn't to guilt fathers into staying home. You are working abroad because you are among the best and brightest at what you do. Corporations or the military have brought you overseas, expecting and anticipating considerable benefits from your talents and energies. For some men, however, the pressure to work longer hours often comes not from their employers, but from within themselves.

Nurturing a family requires us to make proactive, deliberate, and willful choices regarding the use of our time. This may include passing up the big promotion that would require additional time away from home. Don't fall for the fallacy that you can make up time with the family over the next holiday. Life is mostly lived in the mundane. It's those day-to-day experiences that leave the indelible impressions. How we invest our time with our spouse and children during these critical years is more of a testimony to who we are than any job title ever could be.

Lacking Significant Friendships with Other Males

One thing we men aren't particularly good at is discussing with others what goes on in our inner-lives. Cultural and media influences have embedded in our psyche the notion that real men don't need genuine friendships. Occasionally, however, an intro-spective writer like Henry David Thoreau comes along and notes with eloquence the true state of our condition: "Most men lead lives of quiet desperation and go to the grave with the song still in them."[1]

Men need authentic friendships. At our core, we are rela-tional. There are things going on in our lives that our wives won't understand, can't empathize with, and maybe won't even comprehend. (This statement is true for woman, as well.) Men, do you have one or two guys who know the real you? Friends who can call your bluff when necessary and hold you account-able when you are contemplating actions that could harm the relationship you have with your spouse and children? Fortunate is the man who has friends like this, for we are not meant to take on life alone.

FAQs

What marriage advice would you offer to couples as they work, live, and raise a family overseas? I am not by formal training a marriage counselor. Having said this, I've worked enough with parents over the past twenty years that I have observed common marital patterns that are toxic. These include keeping score, refusing to change, trying to "fix" a spouse, not cultivating a friendship with your spouse, and not purposefully carving out relationship time.

Let's face it, raising a family is a difficult undertaking, much more so for parents who are intentional about this work. Without consistent time set aside to work on relationships, life continues to happen. The question isn't, "will our mar-riage/relationship grow;" it's "will we grow together?" What kind of relationship do you want after the kids leave the nest? Working back from your agreed-upon answer, figure out what you need as a team to reach it. Then be proactive to make it happen in the present.

What suggestions do you have for men who travel frequently? Accountability is key. Having other men in your life whom you can trust, who can come alongside you and who can ask questions regarding your actions and behaviors is essential for keeping one's path clear of the temptations and enticements. I know some men who have accountability partners (other men) in cities they travel to most frequently. Knowing you will have to give an account of your time, activities, and engagements creates a hedge of protection. Sadly, many men operate under the lone wolf mentality, believing they can go it alone. Men, having checks and balances in the form of accountability is a necessity. Why? Because you don't *fall* into temptation—it is a slow, almost imperceptible, process.

What are the rates of divorce among expatriates? Statistics on divorce rates among expats vary widely. I've seen figures as high as 60 percent in some online postings; however, I couldn't locate empirical literature to support those assertions. I do know that expats divorce, and do so for similar reasons as the folks back in North America, including infidelity, finances, and the breakdown of communication.

A significant cost for international families centers on the spouse who spends frequent periods of time away. Situations like these can increase the risk factors—high mobility, unstructured time, feelings of anonymity, and sexual enticements. These are all associated with divorce. In certain parts of the world, women (and men) actively seek out international businessmen, propositioning them for sexual liaisons. Some men attempt to justify sexual exploits as harmless, somehow falsely believing they can compartmentalize this part of their life. They can't. In time, these actions will come to light, and when they do, it is at a significant cost to the family.

In what ways is divorce different for expat kids compared to kids who remain in their country of passport? When divorce occurs while living abroad, there can be significant disruptions in kids' lives. Sometimes Mom or Dad will move into a serviced apartment or may even move to another country, leaving the kids and spouse behind. One spouse may take the kids and move back home, or they may leave the kids behind. I've seen all sorts of machinations over the years. There is no real pattern, but there is specific intense pain. In most cases, the company that hired the working spouse covers school fees for the kids. If the spouse who is employed by said company leaves the country, then covered school fees in most cases disappear along with housing costs, flights, shipping fees, and in some cases, the availability to even remain in the country. This results in the left-behind spouse either finding a job in country to cover these costs or covering the costs to return to their country of passport.

What counseling options are available to families going through marital problems? My vague answer: it depends. In some countries, ample and comprehensive counseling services are available. Military families have family services available, providing counseling and guidance. In some countries, however, counseling services are quite limited. Language and cross-cultural difficulties may also make counseling difficult. In such cases, there are online options for counseling. Schools may be able to provide limited counseling support to kids and families, but in most cases, these services wouldn't be comprehensive or protracted.

My kids are asking me why Daddy (or Mommy) is no longer living with us. What should I say? You can be sure questions will arise. It may be tempting to make the cheating spouse pay for what they've done by sharing details with the kids. Sometimes, due to the hurt and shame, parents try to hide their pain, but the kids know something's out of sync. There will be times when kids will ask tough questions that tear at the very heart of a parent. Take a deep breath, sit down with them, and walk them through their feelings. When answering their questions consider your child's developmental age and the story you want them to know.

Your Child's Developmental Age
Children will need different information and ask different questions based on their age and emotional/cognitive maturity. One thing is sure, all kids will need to understand what will happen moving forward—where will they live, will they remain overseas attending the same school, will they have to move to a new home, where will Dad (or Mom) live? The questions won't

all come at once. Initially, there may not be any questions. During these times, however, know that they are listening. You will need to address your kid's perception that somehow they may have caused the divorce. Address this in your conversation with them from the start.

Decide What Divorce Story You Will Communicate

While it may be true, announcing that "Daddy won't be living with us anymore because he's a cheat and had sex with another woman" won't help your child (at any age) deal with the hurt they are experiencing. The offended partner may attempt to get the kids to take sides, rounding up the children in his/her camp and opposing the offending spouse. But keep this in mind: The offending partner will forever be your child's dad or mom. They may lose their position of authority in the home, but they will forever retain this title. A primary contributor to kids adjusting in positive ways is how conflicts between the parents are addressed. As far as it is possible with you, try not to make the kids choose sides.

There are countless relationships affected when divorce occurs. An entirely new parenting paradigm will be established. In some cases, parents can work through the hurt and pain and establish a new normal. In other cases, reconciliation won't be an option. Your kids are going to need the influence of a caring parent, even an offending parent, in their life. Keep these thoughts in mind as you work through this process.

My husband and I are divorcing, not because one of us was unfaithful but because we just don't love one another the way we used to. How do we share this with the kids? A mother asked me this question about an hour before I was scheduled to meet with her thirteen-year-old son. Her son was having difficulties dealing with peers, completing work, and his mood state was low. These weren't his normal patterns of behavior. I began to understand why.

If it is possible, tell the kids you're divorcing when you're together. It is paramount for your kids to understand that, while your relationship with one another is changing, you are both still their parents. How your time will be divided and how their time will be divided will have to be sorted out. As noted earlier, divorce for expat families carries with it a host of unique challenges. You must address these areas with your kids.

Kids and adults will *get through* divorce, but they will never *get over* it. Divorce is a life-changing experience, one with life-lasting implications for kids and adults alike. This is why I strongly encourage parents, as far as it is possible for them, to seek reconciliation. However, holding on solely for the kids' sake isn't a great option either, as it puts tremendous pressure on kids to live up to parental expectations. My advice is to work on your marriage because you want to make your marriage relationship work.

Jake reminded me of this. He is sixteen (grade eleven), and according to him, his parents are "making a go of their marriage for the kid's sake." He describes his home as a hell hole. His parents rarely speak to one another. They spend little to no time together, but they maintain the marriage for the kids. At this point, Jake feels like he's being used as glue, trying to hold things together. When he doesn't perform as expected, he feels tremendous pressure that he will be the underlying cause for his parents' eventual divorce. The reality, however, is that his parents have already split. They are simply carrying out a business transaction and the kids are part of the currency. Separate vacations, sleeping arrangements, and meals are part of their new routine.

Even as divorce becomes increasingly more common, that doesn't mean it is less traumatic. The hurts go beyond description, and life trajectories change significantly. So what can you do for the pain? The primary medicine is time. The scars will remain, but time will promote healing, provide perspective, and allow for growth.

22

I'm Not Finished!

*All...seeds are not perennial;
some of them are like cactuses
blooming only after a long gestation.*

FRED SMITH

Terry struggled throughout high school; he graduated only by the grace of his English teacher changing his grade from an F to a D. Watching him cross the stage to receive his diploma, I reflected on the numerous conversations we'd had with his parents and teachers throughout the year. Terry hadn't met the educational or developmental milestones that indicated he was ready for adulthood, but I knew he would...eventually.

Fast-forward six months. Terry showed up this past week at school. Since graduation, he has been traveling, working, reflecting, planning, and finding himself. He needed a year off before beginning community college to sort out heart issues, to figure out who he is, and to make plans.

As we conversed, Terry commented, "When I was in high school, I knew I could do the work, but I couldn't see the bigger picture as to why I should. I didn't know who I was, what I believed, or even why I believed it. I'm still sorting that out. I guess I'm not finished growing up."

I so enjoy working with kids like Terry. They remind me that life's trajectory isn't a straight line. It is filled with dips, twists, bumps, plateaus, and valleys. If kids persist, they'll have one heck of a ride!

ૐ

Terry's story is my story, maybe even yours. I grew up in a single-parent home. I attended at least ten different schools between kindergarten and twelfth grade and was the only child out of five kids to graduate from high school. You can bet I had gaps in learning. What I lacked in skills, however, I made up for in will—I was determined to learn, to graduate, to move forward. Those formative years shaped my counseling practice and softened my heart for kids who struggle with traditional learning and life journeys. I shared Terry's story with a friend, educator, accomplished author, and public speaker. In response, here is what he wrote:

> There's no way I was ready for college when I was eighteen. I wasn't focused enough, academically. There was a youthful exuberance I needed to get out of my system—one I didn't want to waste doing drinking games (as so many other unprepared kids do) in college. When I eventually went to university, it was only thanks to upgrading courses at a community college. Because I was paying my way, there was no way I was going to fail. At least, that's how I saw it.

> Before getting to university, the last time I had received an A on my report card was in the seventh grade. I went from eighth grade through twelfth without getting a single A. My report card was littered with D grades, and at least two Fs every year. To this day, I only have tenth-grade math (D grade) and an introductory Algebra (another D).

> In contrast, college and university seemed so much easier for me. Kids who did well in my high school trailed my results in college. I graduated "with distinction," which is what it said on my transcript. But I never liked school, not even college or university.... Perhaps Terry and I have plenty in common.
> —Andrew Hallam,
> author of *The Millionaire Teacher* and
> *The Global Expatriate's Guide to Investing*

What's your story? I suspect quite a few readers can relate to Terry's, Andrew's, or mine. Looking back, your high school experience may have held few mountaintop moments. The same may be said for your child at this moment. Still, they may be valley dwellers, attempting to make the ascent to the mountaintop but running out of time. Sure, they're learning, but they are struggling with meeting predetermined timelines (semester grades, graduation, etc.) and this is making you nervous—very nervous. Take heart; at some point, they will make that final ascent. And what will they find at the summit? A vista filled with more mountains and valleys.

Mountaintops, valleys, plateaus, ascents, and descents are all part of life's journey. When kids struggle academically, our focus on matters of the heart should be as thoroughly explored as the academic. After twenty-five years in education (twenty-one of which have been in international schools), I'm convinced that the overwhelming learning issues teens deal with are heart issues—worth, purpose, meaning, value. This isn't to suggest there won't be any corresponding academic issues; there are. But matters of the heart must be addressed first before any significant headway can be made in the books.

Scores of variables affect learning, including motivation, maturation, emotion, cultural transmission (peer influence), and genetics. In Terry's case, it wasn't bad parenting, genetics, or negative peer influences that held him back; it was self-pity. Coming from a divorced family, not hitting academic milestones like other kids, and grappling with self-worth created the perfect recipe for "wallow stew."

Part of the challenge we faced when he came to see me was addressing and validating his feelings and then attempting to develop a plan he could own, but we ran out of time. Terry and I weren't able to work through his issues in time for him to demonstrate he was a responsive and responsible adult; however, our meeting was a wonderful affirmation that he'd get there. There is still more to be sorted, but he is developing the right mindset, surrounding himself with positive influences, and planning and preparing for the future—all healthy markers of adulthood.

Kids don't learn at the same rate or even in the same ways. As a result, not all children learn at high enough levels to meet the standards. Instead, let's declare that all kids can learn! This shifts our focus from the outcome (meeting the standard, earning high marks) to the process (effort, time management, emotional regulation, good decision-making skills). The statement "All kids can learn" acknowledges that life sometimes hits kids square in the face with circumstances bigger than they can handle, and that can result in limited to lackluster output until the matters of the heart, head, and home are sorted out.

The good news is schools are beginning to figure this out. They are coming to understand that matters of the heart are more important than academic ones. (Yes, you read that correctly.) They are learning that providing opportunities for teachers to relate to kids in social and emotional ways is of paramount importance. In school settings, this may take the form of advisory or character education programs. What's important for parents and schools to understand is that, without continued emphasis on matters of the heart, learning progresses at a much slower rate.

I know full well Terry will have additional challenges moving forward. His life's journey is only beginning. Having noted this, however, I am encouraged that he has others in his support network to push, pull, and otherwise motivate him toward his goals. In fact, he recently wrote to me with this encouraging news:

> I will say college [is] difficult, but I've honestly never enjoyed school as much as I do now. I've gone from an F or C student to an A or B student. I've decided to email you now about this because I got an A on my most recent biology test, and the teacher told me it was the highest grade out of both of his biology classes. Thank you for the pep talk before I left Singapore. I found it to be very motivational. It has helped me get through some of my more straining assignments.

If your child is in a season of life where the path forward is unclear, I encourage you to surround them with a network of kind, carrying, and supportive adults. Add to this a supportive peer network, and you can know they will find their way to the summit.

FAQs

We arrived at the start of the school year (ten months ago) but our son, a twelfth grader, continues to struggle. We recognized there would be academic and social adjustments, but this has been going on longer than we anticipated. Now that he is nearing graduation, what are our options? It's downright painful to watch your kids struggle with learning and relationships—painful for the kids, painful for the parents, and painful for the whole family. Sometimes parents question if they are contributing to the problem or if they are the direct cause. They also question what the school is doing to support their child, but that is as far as many parents take their questions. They don't seek out answers. Maybe it's the pace of life internationally or the belief their kid will eventually sort it out. But what happens if they don't? What if the issues continue through the summer and into the start of college?

Some parents find themselves in these situations. Then, with thousands of miles between them and their child at college, they wonder if their child is going to be okay. If this describes the situation you are facing, speak with a representative from the student life center at the college. It is essential for your son/daughter to get connected, find support, and not be left to go it alone. Schools offer a range of services and supports including counseling, support groups, and medical services. It will be important for the student-life counselor to understand what supports have been in place, what structures might be needed going forward, and what might need to be communicated to professors.

It is also important to recognize that your child is now legally an adult. For you to make these requests, your child will have to give consent. Hopefully, you have earned their trust through the years, and they will allow you to continue to advocate on their behalf. It is not uncommon in these situations for one parent to remain near their child for several months until they believe the issues are sorted and he/she is ready to take on school alone.

This might work well when there are no additional children in the home, but what if there are? Knowing your child may not be ready to go it alone even though they are an adult, you may find it necessary to have them attend school near extended family or take some online college courses while still living with you and then have them transfer into a university later.

How kids transition into university is often heavily influenced by how they exit high school. If you note significant academic or social/emotional issues throughout your child's twelfth-grade year, you will need to address these matters before your child heads off to college. If you don't, you may end up doing it during their freshman year at university.

My child was admitted to college, but they aren't ready to attend. What now? Sometimes this happens. It may be a season of life, an illness, or an extended family circumstance that postpones their attendance. Perhaps they need a year off to work, explore options, and contemplate possibilities. It is often possible for kids to request a deferment from university (called a gap year) to sort out some of the issues noted above.

Some parents recognize that sending their child to college in their current condition is tantamount to throwing money away. They've seen marginal maturation through their child's senior year of high school, and they aren't prepared to write a check while knowing there's a good chance the funds won't be put to good use. Parents may need to place expectations on their kids that must be met before funds are provided for school.

It is important to continue asking whether your child is making positive steps toward owning their actions and behaviors. Their trajectory may be out of sync with similar age peers, but hopefully the momentum is moving them in the right direction. If kids do take the year off, as far as it is possible with you, make sure they have a plan. Hanging out in the spare room or basement trying to find the best Wi-Fi signal is not a plan. Having a plan provides stability and predictability. As your teens move into adulthood, they will need to have this as a part of their routine.

Our school/community places a lot of emphasis on elite college acceptance. My daughter believes that if she doesn't get into a top-tier university, her high school efforts were in vain. How should we address this? Sadly, many kids (and parents) have bought in to the lie that "university equals destiny." Some international communities believe only a handful of elite universities can provide an excellent education with post-university opportunities. In reality, there are over six thousand colleges and universities in the United States, not to mention the rest of the world, that offer unique learning environments and opportunities. The college counseling department at my present school does a great job (bias noted) of communicating the message of "right fit," recognizing that every student's unique learning profile contributes to where they should apply. School communities driven by "top-tier university acceptances or nothing" are filled with anxiety, stress, and discord. My advice is to keep the focus on your child and their learning; work closely with your child's college counselor to frame reality.

Can you share about your experience regarding the phrase "winning the college lottery"? I was working with a student who was struggling with anxiety issues tied to the college admissions process. With a 4.25 GPA, multiple advanced placement courses, and a host of extracurricular activities, he figured he was a shoe-in for acceptance at a top-tier university. What he hadn't planned on was thousands of other kids having a similar profile. Upon this realization, he began questioning his efforts and the previous three-and-a-half years of schooling, wondering why he had put himself through all this. Lovingly, his college counselor helped him understand that his efforts had taken him to the front door of the said top-tier universities, but that didn't guarantee admittance. There was a minimum standard he had to meet to get to the door, but beyond this, his chances of admission were a bit of a gamble. To illustrate this, the counselor instructed him to imagine rolling two dice, each consisting of a hundred numbers. To be admitted, he would need to correctly guess which numbers he had rolled. This is akin to what the college admission process has become for highly selective universities.

Some students have a hook that sets them apart from other applicants—a parent with a few hundred million dollars willing to make a substantial donation; a child of a prominent diplomat; an athlete specializing in fencing; a legacy student whose parents, grandparents, and great-grandparents attended; or a student who is the first in his/her family to attend university. These hooks, along with prequalifications like GPA, SAT, ACT scores, letters or recommendations, and extracurricular activities, weigh into the admissions process. The point is, kids may never know all the underlying reasons they are accepted or denied admission, but this doesn't mean their efforts were in vain.

Don't focus here on one or two exclusive universities, believing it is one of these schools or nothing. Your child's university admittance isn't a certainty, but it does mark the beginning of new levels of learning, growth, and opportunities.

ABOUT THE AUTHOR

For the past twenty-two years, Dr. Jeff Devens has worked in international education as a school psychologist, counselor, and classroom educator. (Well, he doesn't call it work. He sees it as getting paid to have fun with kids, colleagues, and parents.) Growing up on public assistance and being the only one in his family of five children to graduate from high school, Dr. Devens has a unique appreciation for the hurt, heartache, and pain teens and families encounter during adolescence. It was the power of loving and caring adults and the grace of God that made the difference for him. Those life experiences during such a formative time shaped his future and practice. Now as he works alongside kids and families with broken hearts, he offers hope, noting, "It's not our circumstances that determine our future, it's our choices."

In his current role at Singapore American School, Dr. Devens works as a school psychologist, counselor, and academic advisor to students, parents, and faculty. In addition, he coordinates the crisis response team, provides talks on mental health, educational, and parenting issues, and writes for school and community publications.

For additional information regarding speaking engagements, conference presentations, teacher/parent workshops, or parenting consultations, please contact Dr. Devens via email or Twitter.

Email: Overseasparenting@gmail.com
Twitter: https://twitter.com/overseasparent

NOTES

Introduction

1 The International School Consultancy. "ISC Reports." ISCresearch.com. July 2017. Accessed September 10, 2017. http://www.iscresearch.com.

2 Custer, Sara. "International Schools Expected To Reach 3.7m Students in 2014." ThePieNews.com. January 14, 2014. Accessed September 18, 2017. https://thepienews.com/news/international-schools-expected-reach-3-7m-students-2014/.

3 "About DoDEA." DoDEA: US Department of Defense Education Activity. August 2015; http://www.dodea.edu/aboutDoDEA/Index.cfm.

Chapter 1: Welcome Home

1 Pollock, David, and Ruth Van Reken. *Third Culture Kids: Growing Up Among Worlds*. Yarmouth, Maine: Nicholas Brealey Publishing/Intercultural Press, 2001.

Chapter 2: Foundations

1 "America's Seven Faith Tribes Hold the Key to National Restoration." Barna.com. April 27, 2009. Accessed February 3, 2017. https://www.barna.com/research/americas-seven-faith-tribes-hold-the-key-to-national-restoration/.

2 Meyer, Stephenie. *Twlight*. The Twilight Saga, Book 1. New York, Boston: Little, Brown and Company, 2005.

Chapter 3: Cornerstones

1 Feldman, Robert. *The Liar in Your Life: The Way to Truthful Relationships*. New York, NY: Hachette Book Group, 2009.

2 "Slander." *Merriam-Webster Online Dictionary*. Springfield, MA: Merriam-Webster, Incorporated, 2015. Accessed August 8, 2016. https://www.merriam-webster.com.

3 Matthew 12:34. Scripture taken from the New King James Version®. Copyright © 1982 by Thomas Nelson. Used by permission. All rights reserved. BibleGateway.com. Accessed September 7, 2017. https://www.biblegateway.com/passage/?search=matthew12:34&version=NKJV.

4 "Responsibility." *Merriam-Webster Online Dictionary*. Springfield, MA: Merriam-Webster, Incorporated, 2015. Accessed August 3, 2016. https://www.merriam-webster.com.

5 "Respect." *Merriam-Webster Online Dictionary*. Springfield, MA:

Merriam-Webster, Incorporated, 2015. Accessed August 5, 2016. https://www.merriam-webster.com.

6   "Fairness." *Merriam-Webster Online Dictionary*. Springfield, MA: Merriam-Webster, Incorporated, 2015. Accessed August 1, 2016. https://www.merriam-webster.com.

7   Brown, H. Jackson. *Life's Little Instruction Book: 511 Suggestions, Observations, and Reminders on How to Live a Happy and Rewarding Life*. Nashville, Tennessee: Thomas Nelson Company, 2000.

8   "Compassion." *Merriam-Webster Online Dictionary*. Springfield, MA: Merriam-Webster, Incorporated, 2015. Accessed September 10, 2016. https://www.merriam-webster.com.

9   Kohler, Kaufmann, and Emil G. Hirsch. "Compassion." JewishEncyclopedia.com. Accessed September 10, 2017. http://www.jewishencyclopedia.com/articles/4576-compassion.

10 Exodus 34:6. *The Holy Scriptures According to the Masoretic Text*. Philadelphia, PA: The Jewish Publication Society of America, 1917.

11 Narada, Mahathera. *The Buddah and His Teachings*. Mumbai, India: Jaico Publishing House, 2006.

12 Al-Jibouri, Yasin. *Allah: The Concept of God in Islam: Volume One*. New York, NY: AuthorHouse, 2012.

13 Mark 6:34. Scripture taken from the The Holy Bible, New International Version®, NIV®. Copyright © 1973, 1978, 1984, 2011 by Biblica, Inc.® Used by permission. All rights reserved worldwide. BibleGateway.com. Accessed September 7, 2017. https://www.biblegateway.com/passage/?search=Mark+6:34&version=NIV.

14 Schopenhauer, Arthur. *The World as Will and Representation, Vol. 1.*, New York: Dover Publications, 1966.

Chapter 4: Fostering an Attitude of Gratitude

1   This quote is most often attributed to John F. Kennedy; however his legislative assistant, Theodore C. Sorensen, disclosed recently (1993) that this saying was found on material that came to him from the New England Council. The motto rang true for Kennedy, and it found its way into many of his speeches. The origin of the quote most likely has roots in fishermen's stories from that area. "Origin of 'A rising tide lifts all boats'." English Language & Usage. February 25, 2015. Accessed May 2017. https://english.stackexchange.com/questions/230520/origin-of-a-rising-tide-lifts-all-boats.

2   Lake, Rebecca. "How Much Income Puts You in the Top 1%, 5%, 10%?" Investopedia.com. September 15, 2016. Accessed March 13, 2016. http://www.investopedia.com/news/how-much-income-puts-you-top-1-5-10/.

Chapter 5: Questioning Faith
1   "From Thomas Jefferson to William Roscoe, 27 December 1820." Founders Online: National Archives and Records Administration. Accessed June 13, 2017. https://founders.archives.gov/documents/Jefferson/98-01-02-1712.
2   "Tolerance." *Merriam-Webster Online Dictionary*. Springfield, MA: Merriam-Webster, Incorporated, 2015. Accessed 15 August 2016. https://www.merriam-webster.com.
3   Von Bergen, C. W., PhD, and George Collier, PhD. "Tolerance as Civility in Contemporary Workplace Diversity Initiatives." Administrative Issues Journal: Connecting Education, Practice, and Research. January 7, 2016. https://aij.scholasticahq.com/article/522-tolerance-as-civility-in-contemporary-workplace-diversity-initiatives.

Chapter 7: The Cost of Comparison
1   Stanley, Sandra. *Comparison Trap: A 28-Day Devotional for Women*. 1st ed. Atlanta, GA, North Point Resources, 2015.

Chapter 9: Doing What Feels Right vs. Doing What Is Right
1   Swindoll, Charles. *Parenting: From Surviving to Thriving*. Nashville, TN: Thomas Nelson, 2006, p. 37.
2   Chapman, Gary. *The 5 Love Languages of Children*. Chicago, IL: Northfield Publishing, 2016.

Chapter 10: How Heartache Produces Hope
1   NOVA: National Organization for Victim Assistance. "Championing Dignity and Compassion for those harmed by Crime and Crisis." Accessed March 14, 2017. http://www.trynova.org.

Chapter 11: Boundaries
1   Cloud, Dr. Henry, and Townsend, Dr. John. *Boundaries*. Grand Rapids, MI: Zondervan, 2007.
2   "Boundary." *Merriam-Webster Online Dictionary*. Springfield, MA: Merriam-Webster, Incorporated, 2015. Accessed 8 October 2015. https://www.merriam-webster.com.

3   Cloud, Dr. Henry and Townsend, Dr. John. *Boundaries.*

Chapter 13: Fully Developed Frontal Lobes: A Parental Dilemma
1   Dekaban, Anatole S., and Doris Sadowski. "Changes in Brain
     Weights during Span of Human Life - Relation of Brain Weights to
     Body Heights and Body Weights." *Annals of Neurology* 4, no. 4
     (October 1978): 345-46.
     https://www.researchgate.net/publication/264680865_Changes_in_
     Brain_Weights_during_Span_of_Human_Life_-
     _Relation_of_Brain_Weights_to_Body_Heights_and_Body_Weight
     s.
2   Jha, Paresh. "Experts: Teen Brain Not Fully Developed by the
     Time They Start Driving." NewCannonNewsOnline.com. June 6,
     2012. Accessed March 28, 2016.
     http://www.newcanaannewsonline.com/news/article/Experts-Teen-
     brain-not-fully-developed-by-the-3614336.php.
3   Jensen, Frances E., and Amy Ellis Nutt. *The Teenage Brain: A
     Neuroscientist's Survival Guide to Raising Adolescents and Young
     Adults.* Toronto, Ontario, Canada: HarperCollins, 2016.

**Chapter 14: Fostering Responsibility and Independence in
Children and Teens**
1   Kann, Laura, PhD. "Youth Risk Behavior Surveillance—United
     States, 2015." *Centers for Disease Control and Prevention:
     Morbidity and Mortality Weekly Report* 65, no. 6 (June 10, 2016).
     https://www.cdc.gov/healthyyouth/data/yrbs/pdf/2015/ss6506_upd
     ated.pdf.

Chapter 15: From Teenagers to Screenagers
1   Ruston, Delaney, MD. ScreenagersMovie.com. 2016. Accessed
     June 17, 2017. https://www.screenagersmovie.com.
2   "Kids & Media @ the New Millennium." KFF.org (The Henry J.
     Kaiser Family Foundation). October 31, 1999. Accessed
     September 18, 2015. http://www.kff.org/hivaids/report/kids-media-
     the-new-millennium/.
3   Wexberg, Steven, Dr., and Elizabeth Hellerstein, Dr. "Can Teens
     Learn While Multitasking?" YourTeenMag.com. January 17, 2017.
     https://yourteenmag.com/teenager-school/is-multitasking-helpful-
     or-harmful-to-teenagers.
4   Bart, Mary. "Turnitin Study Shows Impact of Plagiarism
     Prevention and Online Grading at Higher Education Institutions."
     FacultyFocus.com. February 5, 2014. Accessed January 13, 2016.

https://www.facultyfocus.com/articles/edtech-news-and-trends/turnitin-study-shows-impact-plagiarism-prevention-online-grading-higher-education-institutions/.

5   Bates, Daniel. "The Age of the 'Mobile Data Tsunami': How teenage girls send or receive almost 4000 Text Messages a Month." DailyMail.com. December 16, 2011. Accessed December 20, 2016. http://www.dailymail.co.uk/news/article-2075129/The-age-mobile-data-tsunami-How-teenage-girls-send-receive-4-000-text-messages-month.html.

6   Watson, Richard. *Future Minds: How the Digital Age Is Changing Our Minds, Why This Matters, and What We Can Do about It.* London: Nicholas Brealey, 2011, p. 13.

7   Ibid., 163.

8   Shorter, Gillian. "Assessing Internet Addiction Using the Parsimonious Internet Addiction Components Model: A Preliminary Study." *International Journal of Mental Health and Addiction* 12, no. 3 (2014): 351-66. Accessed December 24, 2016. http://hdl.handle.net/1854/LU-6888819.

Chapter 16: Game On

1   Leland, John. "The Gamer as Artiste." *The New York Times*, December 4, 2005. http://www.nytimes.com/2005/12/04/weekinreview/the-gamer-as-artiste.html.

2   Minotti, Mike. "Video Game Software Sales Estimated to Hit $98 Billion by 2020." VentureBeat.com. October 19, 2016. Accessed October 25, 2016. https://venturebeat.com/2016/10/19/video-game-software-sales-estimated-to-hit-98-billion-by-2020/.

3   Kutz, Steven. "NFL took in $13 billion in revenue last season—see how it stacks up against other pro sports leagues." MarketWatch.com. July 2, 2016. Accessed June 17, 2017. http://www.marketwatch.com/story/the-nfl-made-13-billion-last-season-see-how-it-stacks-up-against-other-leagues-2016-07-01; and
Takahashi, Dean. "Worldwide game industry hits $91 billion in revenues in 2016, with mobile the clear leader." VentureBeat.com. December 21, 2016. Accessed June 17, 2017. https://venturebeat.com/2016/12/21/worldwide-game-industry-hits-91-billion-in-revenues-in-2016-with-mobile-the-clear-leader/.

4   Beck, John C., and Mitchell Wade. *Got Game: How the Gamer Generation Is Reshaping Business Forever.* Boston, MA: Harvard Business Review Press, 2006, p. 11.

5   Wallace, Patricia. *The Psychology of the Internet.* New York, NY: Cambridge University Press, 2001, p. 358

6   Becker, David. "Games Junkies—Hooked on 'Heroinware'?" ZDNet.com. April 12, 2002. Accessed June 17, 2017. http://www.zdnet.com/article/games-junkies-hooked-on-heroinware/.

7   Lenhart, Amanda. "Teens, Social Media & Technology Overview 2015." PewInternet.org. April 9, 2015. Accessed November 22, 2015. http://www.pewinternet.org/2015/04/09/teens-social-media-technology-2015/.

8   "Most popular social media sites." Statista. 2017. Accessed September 1, 2017. https://www.statista.com/statistics/199242/social-media-and-networking-sites-used-by-us-teenagers/.

9   Bates, Daniel. "The Age of the 'Mobile Data Tsunami': How teenage girls send or receive almost 4,000 Text Messages a Month." DailyMail.com. December 16, 2011. Accessed December 20, 2016. http://www.dailymail.co.uk/news/article-2075129/The-age-mobile-data-tsunami-How-teenage-girls-send-receive-4-000-text-messages-month.html.

10   White, Martha C. "More Colleges Are Cyber-Stalking Students During the Admissions Process." Time.com. March 9, 2016. Accessed June 17, 2017. http://time.com/money/4252541/colleges-facebook-social-media-students-admissions/.

Chapter 17: Stressed Out

1   "What Is Stress?" Stress.org. January 4, 2017. Accessed March 30, 2017. https://www.stress.org/what-is-stress/.

2   Miller, Thomas W. *Handbook of Stressful Transitions across the LifeSpan.* New York, NY: Springer New York, 2010.

3   Lenhart, Amanda. "Teens, Social Media & Technology Overview 2015." PewInternet.org. April 9, 2015. Accessed November 22, 2015. http://www.pewinternet.org/2015/04/09/teens-social-media-technology-2015/.

4   Lythcott-Haims, Julie. *How to Raise an Adult: Break Free of the Overparenting Trap and Prepare Your Kids for Success.* New York: Saint Martin's Griffin, 2016.

Chapter 18: Can, Should, Cost: Understanding Testing Accommodations for AP/SAT/ACT

1   "Other Disabilities." Collegeboard.org. 2014. Accessed July 18, 2016. https://www.collegeboard.org/students-with-disabilities/documentation-guidelines/other-disabilities.

Chapter 19: Why Alcohol and Teens Don't Mix

1   Johnston, Lloyd D., Patrick M. O'Malley, Richard A. Miech, Jerald G. Bachman, and John E. Schulenberg. "2016 Overview: Key Findings on Adolescent Drug Use." Monitoringthefuture.org. December 13, 2016. Accessed January 12, 2017. http://monitoringthefuture.org/pubs/monographs/mtf-overview2016.pdf.

Chapter 20: Know the Signs of Suicide

1   Centers for Disease Control and Prevention. "Welcome to WISQARS™ (Web-based Injury Statistics Query and Reporting System)." CDC.gov. January 12, 2017. Accessed April 15, 2017. https://www.cdc.gov/injury/wisqars/index.html#.

2   Centers for Disease Control and Prevention. "Suicide: Facts at a Glance." CDC.gov. March 14, 2015. Accessed April 17, 2016. https://www.cdc.gov/violenceprevention/pdf/suicide-datasheet-a.pdf.

3   Sullivan, Erin M., MPH, Joseph L. Annest, PhD, Thomas R. Simon, PhD, Feijun Luo, PhD, and Linda L. Dahlberg, PhD. "Suicide Trends Among Persons Aged 10-24 Years—United States 1994-2012." CDC.gov. March 6, 2015. Accessed April 22, 2017.
     https://www.cdc.gov/mmwr/preview/mmwrhtml/mm6408a1.htm.

4   Nayar, Usha S. *Child and Adolescent Mental Health*. New Delhi: SAGE Publications, 2012.

5   Cozza, Stephen J., Judith A. Cohen, Joseph G. Dougherty, and Harsh K. Trivedi, eds. *Disaster and Trauma*. First ed. Philadelphia, PA: Elsevier, 2014.

6   Salloum, Ihsan M., and Juan E. Mezzich, eds. *Psychiatric Diagnosis Challenges and Prospects*. Hoboken, NJ: Wiley-Blackwell, 2009.

7   France, Kenneth, PhD. *Crisis Intervention: A Handbook of Immediate Person-to-Person Help*. Sixth ed. Springfield, IL: Charles C Thomas Publisher, Ltd., 2014.

8   Miller, David N. *Child and Adolescent Suicidal Behavior: School-Based Prevention, Assessment, and Intervention.* New York, NY: The Guilford Press, 2011, p. 14.
9   Levine, Madeline, PhD. *The Price of Privilege: How Parental Pressure and Material Advantage Are Creating a Generation of Disconnected and Unhappy Kids.* New York, NY: HarperCollins, 2008.
10 Benard, Bonnie, and Kathy Marshall. "Protective Factors in Individuals, Families, and Schools: National Longitudinal Study on Adolescent Health Findings." *Resilience Research for Prevention Programs*, 2012. http://www.nationalresilienceresource.com/CAPT_Protective_Factors_in_Individuals_F_2012.pdf.
11 Center for Substance Abuse Treatment (US). Trauma-Informed Care in Behavioral Health Services. Rockville (MD): Substance Abuse and Mental Health Services Administration (US); 2014. (Treatment Improvement Protocol (TIP) Series, No. 57.) Chapter 3, Understanding the Impact of Trauma. Available from: https://www.ncbi.nlm.nih.gov/books/NBK207191/ Accessed June 17, 2017.
12 "The Selfie Obsession." Netsanity.net. Accessed February 4, 2017. https://netsanity.net/kids-taking-selfies/.
13 Salloum, Ihsan M., and Juan E. Mezzich, eds. *Psychiatric Diagnosis Challenges and Prospects.* Hoboken, NJ: Wiley-Blackwell, 2009.
14 Nayar, Usha S. *Child and Adolescent Mental Health.* New Delhi: SAGE Publications, 2012.

Chapter 21: A Letter to Husbands
1   Thoreau, Henry David. *Civil Disobedience and Other Essays.* United States: BN Publishing, 2009.